A

Kaleidoscope

Of love

BY J.R. MACK

Contents

I Dedicate...

First and foremost, I want to thank everyone who has chosen to take the time out of their day to consider reading this book. It's taken me a long time to complete it but I have finally done it. I would like to thank all of my friends and family who have supported me throughout the last 10 years (yes, that's how long it's taken me to finish) and have been on this roller coaster journey with me.

I would like to dedicate this book to my BEAUTIFUL black Princesses: Melody-Rion Tiarrah Mack and Lyric-René Joyce Mack. These two girls are the reasons that I wake up every day, their mom Tawanna, thank you so much for listening to me continuously get excited talking about this project. I love you.

Additionally, this is dedicated to my father, William Mack Jr., who is no longer with us in the physical but he is definitely present in the spirit; and my beautiful mother, Brenda. This is the lady that I get my attitude from so when you hear me talk, know that it's her coming out. LOL. I love you past the end of the earth. My siblings: Alecia, Anthony, Terrence, Del, Kim, JJ... I love y'all asses. My cousins: Aminah, Dawnisha, Tanei, Rashida, and Tiffany, a.k.a. my twin... y'all know the love is real. All of my Aunts, Uncles, nieces, and nephews.

My Turner Job Corps (TJCC) family: Cina, Shenia, Ashley, Omari, Dyasunia, Ms. Shedrick, Angela, Pookie, and everyone else studying Culinary Arts from 2005-2006. These people have been there through some of the toughest times and situations in my life and I can't thank them enough. Drina, Patrice J., Patrice B. and my Godson Micah, Liz, Markisha and my Goddaughter Xavia, Henry, Bianca, Chelle, Erika L., Erica P., Erika E., Ella, Parell, Gail and let's not forget, Lawrence, who supported it from the time it was just handwritten in my Five-star notebook lol. Last but not least, I want to dedicate this book to the memory of Tommy D. Crooks, Raylawn Woods, and my cousin, Toyian R. Williams. I really love and miss you guys. Rest in Peace to all of you.

Thanks everyone for the love, support, patience, and the sincere motivation. I love and appreciate all of you without end. I hope I've made you proud. This is not only my dream; it's OUR dream. Enjoy!

P.S. I want to thank my ex's…YES! This book would not have existed if you all hadn't put me through hell. When you read this, you will know exactly who your character is.

Disclaimer!!

The following story is fact and based on actual people and events. Names have been changed to protect the guilty. Reading discretion is advised…

Chapter 1

"The Good, The Bad, and The Trifling"

Today has been an okay day. All I've been doing is cleaning up and talking on the phone with my best friend of five years, Lisa. We met in ninth grade math class. She wanted to get with me but I turned her down because I said that her lips weren't big enough. Now that we have been friends for so long, we can look back on that and laugh. We're more like brother and sister now…I love her and would do anything for her.

So, we were just shooting the breeze, you know, talking about a little bit of everything, when unexpectedly the mood changed. All of a sudden, she had a mellow tone to her voice and that's when she opened up.

"I have a confession. I still have strong feelings for you and I want to be with you."

"Lisa, get out of here. Stop playing."

"I'm so serious. I've never stopped liking you. I really do care about you. Yea, I know I have a boyfriend and you're seeing someone…but I can't help it."

I had no idea what to think at this point but it doesn't matter because she goes on to say that if she does become single, then she would definitely try her hardest to get with me. It felt good to hear someone want me so badly, but I wasn't too sure if I wanted to take it there. I would hate to ruin a friendship if things didn't work out.

Let me back it up a little bit.

In March of 2004, I told Lisa that I had broken up with someone that I was seeing and how I was ready to get with somebody new. That's when she told me about a friend of hers named Ericka, who was going through some things with her boyfriend. She said that Ericka was ready to leave him and she thought that we would make a good couple. I told Lisa that I wouldn't mind getting to know her. You know, just to see what would happen.

I gave Ericka a call and it rang several times but no one answered.

There was no voicemail or anything! What kind of person doesn't have voicemail in 2004? So, I waited about 20 minutes later to call back and she was there. Yes!!

We talked for nearly three hours about everything. From that point on, we knew we wanted to be with each. We talked and hung out every opportunity we got. I was really feeling her but it seemed that her loyalty was torn. She didn't want to admit it but I knew that there was someone stopping us from being together... her boyfriend, Steve.

"You know I can't keep doing this, right? I can't... Let me rephrase that, I won't be the other man. Never have. Never will."

"You're not the other man. I told you that already."

"Don't play dumb, Ericka. I KNOW you still talk to Steve. But that shit ends today. Understood?"

"Yea," she retorted with a slight attitude. *"I will tell him not to call again when I think he is off work."*

"Alright then. You love me?"

"Negro no! I barely like you," she said with a dimpled grin.

I puckered my lips for a kiss and she kissed me back.

Weeks go by and I cannot describe how much I love Ericka but it just pisses me off when she wants to talk about the things she has done with other guys. She likes to tell me the how, the when, and the how long…Tell me, is it a good idea to listen to her past so in her words I can "get to know her better" or every time she brings it up, just get an attitude like I have been doing? I am honestly trying to do better but I just can't listen to the stories she wants me to listen to. She goes into very graphic, and to me, disrespectful details.

Ericka still talks to most of her ex's and I am not cool with that shit at all! She says that they are all just good friends. Humph. Ain't nobody that good of a friend! For example, when we are on the phone together, she would click over to talk to one of her ex's and forget I am on the damn phone. When I call her out on it, she gets very apologetic and thinks that giving me head will make it all better. Well, it doesn't. I am better than that.

Not to mention, she still tolerates Steve punk ass. The other day Ericka said he showed up at her job with a bouquet of pink roses. What I asked her and myself was *"Why in the hell would a dude come to your job to bring you roses? And the better question, why did you accept them?"*

"I don't know, Jah. I didn't think it was a big deal. It won't happen again. Damn."

She is constantly giving her number to different dudes, saying that they are just cool, just friends. Then she throws in the fact that they all supposedly know about me. Then, why in the hell don't I know anything about them? That just lets me know that I need to have a back-up plan in case this relationship fails…which I know that it will if she continues this bullshit.

A week before prom, Ericka asked, *"Jah, will you take me to the prom?"*

"Nope. When I asked you if you wanted me to go with you, you said no."

"If you aren't going to take me, I have no one to go with…Can Steve take me?"

"You must be out your damn mind if you think that I'm going to be ok with that...hell no."

"I figured that you would say no so I already asked him and he said yea. He also wants to get a room afterwards, is that ok? I mean, it won't just be us. We're going as a group with some of my other friends."

"Ericka, you do what the hell you want to do. It doesn't even matter...have fun." I hung up. She said that I was acting jealous but that's not it. I'm not stupid. I'm not a fool in love and I won't be taken for one either.

The day of the prom, she was supposed to come over. I called her three times just to make sure that she was still coming over. I was out job hunting and just wanted to be sure I was home when she got there. When I finally reached her, she told me to make sure that I was home by a quarter to five. I couldn't wait to see her so I could tell her how beautiful she was.

Well, 5:30 comes around and no Ericka. Five forty-five comes and still no Ericka. And guess who is still waiting? Me! So the next time I looked at my clock it was 6:30 and I was pissed off by then.

I called her and she had the nerve to say, *"I was running too late to stop by. I am getting into the limo now... I'm sorry."*

"What do you mean sorry?" I couldn't hide the aggravation I was feeling. *"Babe, are you serious?"*

She did not answer my questions so I hung up the phone and just laid across the bed.

All of a sudden my heart starts to beat at a rate that even long, deep breaths could not control. I called the only person who could bring me back to my senses and help me get my mind off the whole situation, Lisa. Before I had the chance to even start my story, Lisa asked, *"What's wrong?"* and I started crying.

"What did Ericka do?"

I didn't respond.

"You better call her and tell her it's over!"

I just couldn't hear what she was saying after that because the sound of my heart breaking was too loud.

I was on my way out of the bathroom when my mother told me that Ericka had called, (actually, she said "Miss Tang-A-Lang." She wasn't very fond of Ericka) and I said *"I don't care. She will be okay."* I got on the phone with Lisa and we were watching television in silence; except for the occasional " *Are you okay?"* coming from Lisa. I returned Ericka's call about an hour and a half later... realizing that her phone was off because it went straight to voicemail. I got mad again because every time I called, I got her voicemail. When the voicemail didn't come on, she (or somebody) would answer the phone and hang it right up. Finally, she picked up the phone and we talked. The way she was talking didn't sound right. She almost sounded annoyed that I had called. Wait the hell up, she had a tone that said "I'm trying to get a nut, what do you want?" I bet you are wondering how I know that tone. Well, I will just say that I've had her speak in that tone before.

I asked her what was going on and she said nothing. It was hard for me to believe her because I would occasionally hear faint moans and when I asked her about it, she said that she was just sighing because she was tired. Still being doubtful, I told her that I believed her simply because if something did happen, who would tell anyway? Ericka had started to say things like *"Why don't you trust me?"* and *"Why don't you believe me?"*

"I trusted you before and what did you do?"

Nevertheless, eventually Ericka, her mom, and her sister stopped by my house on prom night. I went outside, with an attitude of course, and told her that she looked nice. She had on a yellow dress and she really did look good but I couldn't enjoy her beauty at that moment because I was still so mad.

Almost instinctively she says, *"I didn't do anything baby. I love you,"* before she got back into the car.

"Okay. Whatever," I retorted as I walked off.

Ericka told me that she was going to call me when she got home because she was very tired and she hadn't eaten anything. So of course I waited, and waited, and WAITED...

Well, I am glad I didn't hold my breath because as you could probably tell, she didn't call. I used to trip but I realized that is pointless. This is just Ericka's M.O. That's just what she does. For example, while we are on the phone, she would get a beep telling her she had a call waiting; she'd tell me she would call me back - but she never did. Or, I'd call her and she would be asleep... well, that is what she says. But I know, I have been on the phone with Ericka and she would get a call from someone she didn't want to talk to, and she would pretend like she was sleep as well. So, who knows if she was blowing smoke up my ass or not. Maybe, she just didn't want to talk to me either. I admit that I am a deep thinker, sometimes too deep, but I know how to read between the lines and not make myself look like a damn fool.

Ericka called saying how she still wants to marry me and have my children but I told her I'm not even trying to get down with her like that until she looks like she is making a change. Sometimes I swear she acts like she was dropped on her head as a baby or something. She may not be bi-polar but her actions sure as hell are. She's still going out giving her number to guys but at the same time saying how she wants to be with me exclusively. What kind of sense does that make?

Okay, now it is the day after the prom and I called Ericka to talk about what went on yesterday and how I felt. The only thing she seemed concerned with was the fact that Lisa told me to break up with her. Why the hell is she so hung up on Lisa and what Lisa said? It's almost like she isn't listening to me or that she gives two fucks about my feelings. Not once did she ask if I was going to break up with her or not.

"Why are you letting Lisa come between us?"

"This isn't about Lisa Ericka. This is about us. Take that back… this is about me and I really just don't want to do this anymore. I can't stop you from doing you, so I am gone! Finished! That's it."

"Jah, are you serious?" she questioned but continued without waiting for a response. *"I really don't want to break up. How about we separate for*

a little while? You know, take some time to calm down and…"

She went silent. I held the line for a second… I guess the part of me that still loved her wanted to hear that I was wrong about what I was thinking or feeling.

She didn't say anything. I really didn't want to break up with her but that's what I had to do in order for me to truly feel better. In actuality, the moment it escaped my lips I started to feel better. I hear people say that "the truth hurts," but in this case, the truth was liberating because I was finally being truthful and real with myself. Don't get me wrong, Ericka and I had a lot of good times but all the extra stuff we went through just wasn't worth it. I really didn't want to be here anymore (meaning the relationship).

A couple of weeks ago, my homeboy Taejon and I went over to Lisa's house. At that time, Ericka and I were not talking because I felt that she had some growing up to do. Now Tae is my boy, but he does some real shady shit, like trying to get with my ex's and telling them that I ain't got to know or telling Ericka something that I had told his stupid ass not to say. I never thought that he would be that kind of a person. Me and Taejon were on Lisa's porch and I was arguing via text with Ericka. I didn't have my phone so I was using his. I got fed up so I gave him back his phone and I went home. Later on that night, Ericka called. She told me some things that I had told Taejon in private and he had sworn to secrecy. The more Ericka talked the more pissed off I became. Taejon had just bumped himself up to #1 on my shit list! Then, to add stank to the shit, Ericka said he was trying to holler at her. Now, how stupid can he be? Somehow the thought came to my mind that I should see how trifling Taejon really was so I got Ericka to text him.

"What's up?"

"Nothing. What's up with me and you?"

I was telling Ericka what to send him and he just fell right into it. He was saying how he was looking at how fat her pussy was whenever he would take me to see her, and how when they get together that I didn't have to know cause it won't be any of my business.

Now, let me just add that Taejon hated Ericka when we were together; calling her bitches, saying how ugly she was, talking about the gap in her teeth, and how skinny she was. If she was so ugly when we were together, why does he want to get with her when we are not together? He should've come back with something like *I can't do that because Jah is my boy* or *why would you even want to fuck around knowing that Jah is my friend?* So now you can just about see how shady, trifling, scandalous, and fake he really is. Taejon was putting pussy before friendship and he proved just how much I don't need him.

Now the time has come for me to call him out on what he's been saying to Ericka. I called him and asked him what was up with the things he has been sending Ericka.

"What you talking about? What messages?"

Oh my God! This dude is not serious. "Taejon, you know what I was talking

20

about!"

That's when he finally admitted to saying those things. But he didn't take the blame, he tried to put it off on Ericka; which I already assumed that he would try and do. The whole time he was on the phone calling her bitches and everything else. I didn't have the heart (at first) to tell him that she was on three-way and she had been listening this whole time. So finally I told her to start talking and that's when he wants to start asking all kinda questions.

"Why ya'll set me up? Ya'll think ya'll all that? Ya'll think ya'll better than everybody?" We just let him talk. When he realized he was caught, all he could say was, *"Yeah, I said that stuff. What did you expect? I'm a nigga!"*

That's when I damn near lost it. That meant that if he had the chance to get with Ericka, he would have done it and not even thought twice about it. He kept on trying to convince me that he never wanted to "get" with her, he was just telling her anything. He also said if he did want her, all she could do was give him head.

Ericka despises Taejon and wants nothing to do with him. And hell, I just don't trust him. How can I be friends with someone I don't trust? I'm not fake so I'm not going to be smiling in his face and then talking behind his back. That's just not me. So, yes! I'm officially saying it... I don't like that bitch and we are not cool. My mother and my brother Jocq said that I shouldn't end the friendship. But how can I be friends with someone that I just don't trust anymore?

I have to be honest and tell you that I have not had feelings for Ericka in a long, long time. She says one thing but her actions said another and I was tired of it and everyone knew except her. My closest friends and family think I should just let this thing with Ericka go. We have been through too much stuff. I think that I will agree with them on this one. I love her but I've just been taking it one day at a time. She and I should really come to some sort of a resolution about this so called relationship.

Mood today? Pissed the hell off. It is always some bullshit Ericka is telling me after the fact.

Like the time she cheated on me before with someone named Frederick. I found this out three weeks after it happened. Her whole reason for doing it was just messy and classless. It happened on a Saturday night after a gospel comedy show at her church. She asked me if I was coming and I said that I was gonna try very hard. I really did want to go but I didn't have a way to get there. After the show was over, she called me from the church parking lot and we talked for a few minutes before she said that she would give me a call back. She later told me that when we got off the phone, she wanted some head so she called Frederick to come pick her up from church.

"The truth is…we went back to his place and had sex. We gave each other head…and….we had actual intercourse. It was unprotected BUT I didn't give myself, or him, the chance to cum."

I couldn't believe the shit I was hearing so I sat in stunned silence and she continued to talk.

"I mean, in the middle of it, I just made him stop because I couldn't stop thinking about you."

"Well, hell… Thank you. I appreciate the fact of you thinking about me while you're fucking someone else. That is so damn considerate. Too bad you weren't thinking about my ass when you got the urge for some head in the parking lot." I replied sarcastically.

She almost sounded sorry when she replied, *"You're right…"*

"Damn right, I'm right."

"I just wasn't thinking at the time. Jah, I really do feel bad now and I felt bad then. After that, I just asked him to take me home."

I didn't say nothing.

"I think I made him feel bad because I couldn't explain to him why I stopped. It was a really long ride home. I was just very quiet because I could not believe what happened."

"Why are you just now telling me this, Ericka?"

"I just couldn't face you knowing that I had cheated."

I should have let her go then but I didn't. You know the old saying,

"Once a cheater always a cheater." I don't know who said it but maybe they were on to something. I know that my suspicions of her are in overdrive. This is too much stress for a relationship. Always wondering if your mate will be faithful.

Today she told me she met someone named "New Orleans" at her job a few days ago. Let me back it up and tell you how I really found out. We were on the phone and her line beeped. She clicked over and just left me hold on. At the ten minute mark, I finally hung up and called her right back. There was no answer but I didn't trip. I asked her about it the next day.

"Oh, that was my friend, New Orleans."

So I asked her where they met at and she said at her job.

"Why did you give him your number?"

"Because I wanted to, Jah. Me and him started talking and exchanged numbers. That's it."

I asked her about their conversation. She said that I was just being nosey and I needed to mind my own business. All I did was ask her what was so captivating about their conversation that she didn't feel the need to beep back over and tell me bye, good night, fuck you... nothing! I mean, let me know what's really good.

"Ericka, you need to get your priorities together."

"What are you talking about?"

"Why do you always act stupid? I'm talking about this New Orleans dude. What the fuck is up with that? I think that shit needs to end. How do you just give some random dude your number and start having conversation with him when you're in a relationship?"

"You're making it into more than it needs to be. We are friends... like you and me are friends."

"Friends?" I interjected with a huff. I guess she fucks all her friends.

"Jah, I am going to do what I want to do... whether you like it or not."

"You are right Ericka, as well as crazy, and I don't even care about having a friendship, or relationship, or really anything else with you."

"Okay."

"Alright, Ericka. At least now we are clear. I am telling you, without a

doubt, that I don't care no more about the relationship we used to have. You are the reason for that relationship being tainted because you were the one being dirty."

I love her and I'm hurt by her actions. I am just tired of trying to get Ericka to understand that I don't need her to make me feel good. I was fine before her and I will definitely be fine without her... definitely. I need to be treated with respect and taken more seriously and she just doesn't seem to get that. I believe once Ericka realizes that she lost me, she will start to regret the things that she has done and understand that she is not the only one who can make me happy.

It's about time to let this one loose. I confess. There was someone else I wanted to get to know romantically if the relationship with Ericka didn't work out. She was a very good friend that I had known since the 5th grade and I started having feelings for in the 7th grade. Her name is Kerala. I realized that I have deep feelings for her when I started having dreams about her lately. I know that she feels the same because she has been giving little hints and a close friend of hers' confirmed it.

Jocq and Lisa think that I was wrong for feeling the way I did about Kerala while I was still dealing with Ericka. They seem to dismiss the fact that I knew Kerala long before Ericka came into the picture. Kerala and I just never acted on what we were feeling. I can't help how I felt and/or feel about Kerala. I mean, how can I truly be happy when Ericka made it damn near impossible to trust her? Now that we are not together, I'm the happiest I've ever been. Ericka is only seventeen and I am nineteen. I knew that she wasn't ready for a serious relationship and neither was I (or maybe I was), but I didn't have to be a damn genius to realize that she didn't love me to the magnitude that I loved her. That is one of the reasons I ended it because I felt that I was loving too much and she was not loving enough. That was probably because I was too nice to her. I damn near changed my whole attitude because of her. I basically dogged everyone that I was with before her but with her I felt like I couldn't treat her any kind of way. For the first time, I cared about the feelings of the person I was with more than my own. There were so many times that I wanted to break up with Ericka but for some reason I couldn't do it. I could never bring myself to let her know how I really felt.

Keeping my feelings bottled up inside eventually took its toll on me. Emotionally, I would pretend to be happy around people when I really wasn't but then go in my room and suffer in silence. Physically, I didn't want to do anything. I didn't want to get out of bed at all. I had stopped exercising as much as I did before. I had started trying to lose weight by not eating as much; but now, I had almost stopped eating period. Mentally, I was not in the right state of mind. I had gotten to the point I was suicidal.

Due to a previous finger infection, I had a prescription for Percocet to deal with the pain. I had a few left; five to be exact, so I took them all. I started to hallucinate, seeing myself outside of my body, laughing at myself and the condition I was in. At the same time, the hallucinations were not allowing me to see myself, but my friends and family, even Ericka. There were other times that I had tried to commit suicide and the way I had planned on killing myself was right in my face but I couldn't go through with it.

I'm glad that I didn't because suicide only makes things worse. When you are in that state of mind you're only thinking about yourself and your pain at that particular time. You have to think about all of the pain and hurt that you will cause your family and friends. It is not worth it and now I am at peace with myself. That next morning I woke up, and I was so mad that I began to cry. I was mad that I was not dead when I felt that I should have been. Now I still have to deal with this thing called life.

A couple of weeks ago, I noticed a nasty bump on my lip, and the corner of my mouth. The first thing that I thought about was herpes. Ericka and I had unprotected vaginal and oral sex. The crazy thing is that we had sex maybe a month before the bumps showed up so the thought of herpes left my mind slightly. That was until I remembered a conversation I had with Ericka. We were talking and I forgot what I said exactly but she got real mad.

"That's okay. We will see who's laughing when they find out they got an STD."

"You are one crazy, sick bitch! Who says some shit like that? I know you better stop playing because I could get real homicidal over some bullshit."

She started laughing. Did someone drop this heifer on her head as a baby? She is acting downright dumb right now. How in the hell does she think this shit is funny? People are dying every day and this bitch is laughing.

"I'm just joking, Jah damn!"

"What?!"

"I'm just playing. Stop being so serious."

"Why the hell would you play like that? That is nothing to play with!"

"I just wanted to see how you would react."

The flashback of that conversation made me really think that I had something. I told Lisa about the bumps and the conversation and she was madder about it than I was.

We agreed that I should go find out if it was herpes or some other STD. Lisa also thought it was a good idea that I call Ericka and tell her that she needs to be checked out too.

Why should I tell her to get checked out if I feel that she already knows? I gave her a call anyways. We talked for a bit, making small talk. Just as I said, *"Ericka, I have to talk to you about something important,"* her line beeped.

"I'll have to call you back."

"Okay, but make sure you call me back because this could be serious."

"Yeah, whatever Jah."

I told Lisa about the little conversation and she said Ericka was just a nasty, mean spirited bitch.

Well, Ericka didn't call me back. So, I've decided that when I go to the clinic to find out what these bumps are and they turn out to be herpes, she will live the rest of her life in hell! And the best part (as far as I am concerned) is she won't even know why I'm treating her like shit because I ain't gonna tell her a damn thing about my diagnosis. She is being a bitch but I can be an even bigger one.

I went to the clinic and the bumps turned out to be nothing but a reaction to this new lotion I was using. I am kinda mad because I wanted to have a reason to mess up her life without her even knowing why. I have done some very mean things to some people in my day and I don't regret one thing. Ericka has yet to see the crazy side of me but she will see it.

While Ericka and I were still going together I let her borrow one of my favorite Lil Mo CDs, "Meet the Girl Next Door." She said that she will bring it back in a few days. A few weeks passed and Ericka has not returned my CD. By that time, I had already broken up with her so we weren't really talking as much as we used to. I called her and asked for my CD back.

"Why are you being so petty?"

"Girl, what are you talking about?"

"Is this your excuse for calling me? You gave me the CD but now that we

aren't together all of a sudden you want it back?"

"First of all, I didn't give it to you. I loaned it to you. You were my girl so what I had, you had. But now that you are not my girl, I want all my shit back. The stuff I gave you, you can keep but my stuff I loaned…well, that's what I am asking for."

"Why can't you let me have it? I want it because it reminds me of you."

I didn't respond.

"I don't understand why we have to end this way. Can we just be friends, Jah?"

"Yea, we can still be friends but I still want my CD."

Then, she had the nerve to tell me she wasn't going to give me my CD back.

So, I let it go for a couple more weeks and I asked for it again and she said that she would bring it over that next Saturday. Saturday came and I didn't hear from her. I called her house and her sister said she was at work, so I waited until about 8 o'clock and called her job. They said that she had already left. I called her house again and no one answered so I left a message. She never called.

I waited another couple days before trying to reach Ericka again.

This time, when I asked to speak with her, her mother said that I couldn't.

"Are you calling about that CD again, Jah?"

"Yes, I am."

"Well, Ericka and her sister were on their way to your house with your CD and they were in a car accident."

"Oh, okay. Well just tell her that I need my CD." I hung up.

I tried everything I could to be nice to Ericka during this breakup. I tried to keep it classy and allow us both to cut our losses without all the extra bullshit. No matter how I tried to end this amicably, she insisted on pushing my buttons. By this point I was done so I had to be the mean, heartless person that I didn't want her to see. I wrote three very explicit letters. One letter was addressed to her mom. It was basically saying what me and Ericka had done, the things Ericka had done before we got together, like the three-some, and that Ericka is a habitual liar. The second one was to her church telling them that she had done things in the parking lot that would make satan blush and that they needed to address the issue with her. Either they needed to preach a sermon about it or pull her aside and let her know. The last letter went to her job. I let them know the things that have happened in the bathroom, in one of the booths in clear view of the customers and in the parking lot. I mailed them off on a Tuesday and her mother got her letter the next day.

Her mother called questioning me about the letter.

"I had nothing to do with it."

"Okay, Jah. But I want you to know that I'm going to have this letter investigated and whoever is behind this letter will be prosecuted."

"O.k. Mrs. Harmon. You can do what you want but you do not have anything on me".

I was very excited and confident because I knew for a fact that there was nothing to investigate. For one, I changed my handwriting. I did not touch the paper or envelope when I was writing so I know there won't be any fingerprints, and lastly, when I was sealing the envelope, I did not lick it. I used water to close it and the mail carrier put the stamp on it so there will be no DNA. To top it all off, I used a fake name and address so that nothing would come back to me.

Soon after that, Ericka called to explain that the reason why I had not gotten my CD the day that she said that she would bring it was because she was in Atlanta. Then, she asked the question I had been waiting for.

"Did you mail a letter to my house?

"No. What are you talking about?"

"Don't act stupid! You are the only one who knew all of my business and all of my ex's! I know you did it because you are so fucking vindictive."

"Ericka, I have no idea what you are talking about."

She hung up the phone. I was dying laughing inside. She then called back and I still denied it. She called me again and apologized saying that she was sorry for accusing me. She was just mad. She also said she was actually blaming every guy that she had ever talked to. I told her it was okay and I forgave her. She then said that she had an idea of who had mailed the letter.

So, she is blaming someone else for something that I did? I'm sorry for that person but I just did what I felt like I had to do. I told her that I can be a bitch and not to mess with me. I feel so good knowing that her mother, pastor, and employer know all of her business. Until this day, she had no idea that it was really me who mailed the letters.

A few days later, my CD arrived by FED-EX. Now that I had my CD, I blocked Ericka from being able to call my phone. Knowing that none of this ever came back to me is hilarious. What do you expect...I'm just that fucking smart!

Chapter 2

"Women are More Confusing than a Man Who Has a Period!"

Kerala and I have a mutual friend named Jasmin. I told her that I like Kerala and she gave me her number. I called Kerala every now and then and I began to realize that the person that I was talking to on the phone was not the one who I saw every day at school. She was just so dead and lame on the phone and everybody knows that I get bored as hell with people quick. We were talking one day about nothing-- as usual and I just said fuck it.

"You know what Kerala? I'm tired of the small talk. I need to tell you the real reason I started calling. I've liked you for a long time now and I want to see if we can expand our friendship to another level.

"Are you serious?"

"Yeah, I didn't start calling you all of a sudden for nothing."

"Why didn't you tell me before now? And why do you like me? How long have you been liking me?

39

"I don't know man."

I finally got tired of all the questions and I told her that I will call her later. I'm sorry but I think I made a mistake by getting that girls number because I'm not interested anymore. I thought she would be different, but I fooled myself because that girl is not somebody that I would ever talk to. I guess my feelings for her weren't that strong after all. It always happens that way. The person that you think you want so badly turns out to be somebody that you end up not liking at all.

Well, now that Kerala is out of my system, I start to think about my friend, Bre'yanna. We've been mad cool since the eighth grade and I always wanted to be with her. She is about 5'6" and real thick. She got a fat ass, big legs, big chest, hazel-green eyes, light-brown complexion, and long hair. Oh yeah, she has my favorite thing on the human body, big lips. This girl is so fine man, it's ridiculous. She never knew, before now, that I liked her. Anyway, when we were in the 11th grade, she got pregnant and I was jealous.

I can't believe that she got with somebody and got pregnant. She had a baby girl the beginning of our senior year and dropped out of school. I don't know if I was more mad or sad that I couldn't see her every day; but, at least, we still talked on the phone. Some time goes by and she is no longer with her baby's father so now I see a chance for me to make my move. We would talk on the phone all night long, until 3 or 4 in the morning and I have to be up at 5:30 for school. We spent a lot of time hanging out at the mall, just riding around, or at her house. Everywhere we went and brought her daughter with us, everyone complemented us on how good our family looks, and how much her daughter looked like me. It was fun hearing people say, *"Ooh, your baby looks just like you."* Or, when Bre'yanna asks me to hold Jameiria, people would say, *"Ooh, I can tell you've got that baby spoiled. She's just gonna be a daddy's girl."* We would laugh about it and walk off.

When we would be on the phone, she would say things that made me think that I had a chance with her like, *"Jah, where are we going take the baby tomorrow?"* One day out of the blue she asked me if there was anything that I wanted to tell her. By her asking me that, I figured that she had to know that I liked her.

"Yeah, there is something that I can tell you, B."

"Well, what is it?"

I beat around the bush for a little while, actually until about 4 in the morning until she finally got tired of me playing around.

"Bre'yanna, I want to be with you."

"Are you serious?"

"Yeah man, I'm serious."

I was scared to hear what she had to say so I just told her that I will call her when I got out of class.

"Okay, make sure you call me back."

That same night I had the most sexual, erotic dream about me and Bre'yanna. She had come to see me and we were in my room laughing, talking or whatever, just chilling. One thing led to another and we were doing some beautiful fucking. It was crazy! I was on my knees eating her pussy while she was backed up against the wall with both her legs hanging over my shoulders. Then she was on all fours on my bed while I was eating her pussy and ass from the back. I then had her on her back with her legs behind her head, fucking her harder than I had ever fucked anyone before. All I could see were those big green eyes looking at me filled with love. We then go in the 69 position and as I am eating and fingering her pussy. She cums all over my face and it was the best. It almost reminded me of when I fucked Ericka... except with Bre'yanna, it was good. That dream felt so real that I woke myself up from it because I heard myself moaning like I was fucking for real.

That next day I couldn't even talk to her. She called me later that night and asked why I hadn't called her all day. I just told her that I was busy. I couldn't tell her how I truly felt. Bre'yanna and I talked for a few more weeks and then all of a sudden the calls stopped. Everywhere I went, I looked for her but she was nowhere to be found.

It finally came to a point that I realized that I had to stop thinking about Bre'yanna. So, I started thinking about a girl that I knew since the ninth grade named Ariyan. She was the cousin of my best friend, Ricardo. She was short, dark-skinned, skinny, and had braces. When we first met, we were real cool. One day, in the middle of class, she tapped me on my shoulder and randomly asked me if I would take her virginity.

"Are you serious, Ariyan?"

"Yes, I am very serious. You look good, we're cool, and I want you to be my first."

I was so fucking excited I damn near fucked her on the spot. My hard dick wanted me to tell her yeah, but my head said no.

"Ariyan, I can't do that. You're my girl, plus my homie's cousin."

"Okay. That's cool, Jah."

That whole class period all we did was talk about sex and the things that we would do and the whole time I was asking myself, *how could you turn down a tight ass pussy like that?* I don't know how I did it, but

I did. We continued to be real good friends after that. About a year later, her mother passed away and Ariyan moved to Philadelphia to live with her sister. By her and Ricardo being cousins, they kept in touch, and he would come back to me saying that she had been asking about me, which made me feel good.

It wasn't until our senior year that I saw her again. She had come back to Georgia and man had she changed. She had a big chest, a big ass, contacts, a new haircut, and no braces. She was somebody that I could definitely fuck now. We talked a little bit in passing but nothing serious. I guess we both had kinda gotten over the past. But I thought I would have enough time to bring it back up....... but I didn't. Not even a month later, she was back in Philly. All I could do was think about how bad I had fucked up again, missing out on what could've been the best girl ever. Ricardo said she's been asking about me and how Ariyan might move back to Georgia. I was excited but I wasn't gonna wait to see if she was coming back. I had to move on.

It is now November 2004 and I finally get back in touch with Bre'yanna after a year. I called and it was like we had never lost contact. We laughed, talked, and reminisced over the past. It felt good being able to talk to her that way again. I guess I got too caught up in how good it used to be that I missed what she said.

"Jah, did you hear me? I said I'm engaged."

I heard that shit this time. My heart dropped.

"Shut up! You're lying!"

"No, I'm serious. I'm getting married in March."

I was already mad that she was engaged and to make matters worse, when I asked her who she was marrying, she replied,

"Who else? My baby daddy."

"Aww, hell nawl. Man, you better be playing."

"Why you think I'm playing? I'm being for real."

She is actually marrying the dude that she wished she would've never gotten pregnant by! How fucked up is that?

"When did ya'll get back together?"

"*Last December,*" she said.

So, all this time I thought that we were getting closer and she got back with this dude instead? Straight bullshit.

"*How long have y'all been engaged, Bre'yanna?*"

"*Since February.*"

As much as I wanted to hold my tongue I wouldn't let myself do it.

"*Bre'yanna, you don't want to marry this dude.*"

"*What would make you think that I didn't want to marry him?*"

"*Well, maybe because…You know what? The reason doesn't matter. Just whatever, man.*"

A few days later I called her. We were talking as usual when she blurts out,

"*Well Jah, I can't have men calling my phone no more.*"

"*Is he paying the bill?*"

"*No, but we are engaged now. We are gonna be a family.*"

"*Well, as long as you pay the damn bill, I will continue to call the phone until you tell me to stop. Do you want me to stop calling you?*"

There was this crazy silence on the phone...

"Yes," she responded in almost a whisper. We talked a little while longer, got off the phone and that was that.

That December, Jasmin, the one who was trying to hook me up with Kerala told me that she wanted to be with me. Now this was weird and in a way nasty because we've been cool since the 6th grade and I never, ever looked at her in that way. As a matter of fact, I always thought that she was gay. She always wore Dickie's and big baggy shirts so why would I be attracted to that? She was still saying that she wanted to get with me and I never gave her an answer because I didn't see her that way nor did I want to hurt her. Jasmin had come over one day on a break from school. She had been asking me to take her virginity and to me that was a very big responsibility, but hey, she was giving up pussy so I said yeah. The day she came over we talked for a minute and then I started finger fucking her. I started off nice and slow with only two fingers. Then I slowly slid a third one inside her and she started moaning. Then, a fourth one and she moaned louder. I rotated my hand to slide my thumb in. My entire first was in! She was the first girl that I ever tried that on. She was breathing heavy and I was getting hard. I leaned down and kissed her in the space between her naval and the top of her pubic hair. She started rotating her hips on my fist and the more she did, the more I wanted to fuck her. I wanted her to cum first so I continued to fist her. A couple minutes go by and I feel what I think is her cumming! Then I start smelling something, so I pulled my fingers out and them shits was bloody.

"Eww get up! You're fucking bleeding on me!"

"Shut up! No, I'm not. Are you serious?"

"Hell yeah, look at my damn hand!" I got up and went to the bathroom, washed my hands, bleached them and then I went back in my room. I sat on the bed. It was quiet for several minutes before she spoke.

"I'm sorry, Jah."

"It's alright man, but that shit was nasty. Guess I popped your cherry huh?"

"I said I am sorry, damn." After a brief pause she said, *"I'm so embarrassed."* She diverted her eyes as she added, *"My first time doing anything and this happened."*

For a brief moment, I almost felt bad for going off on her. I pulled her closer as I laid back and crossed my arms behind my head and said *"don't worry, it happens. I mean, I did have my whole hand in your pussy"*. She laid her head on my chest. After a few moments of lying there in silence, she starts to kiss me on my chest, then eventually my naval...her kisses got lower and lower and my dick became harder and harder. I took a deep sigh. Shit! A brother was really trying hard as fuck not to moan. It felt so damn good. So I pulled it out and she began to suck it. Her mouth was warm— just small. She kept struggling with being able to take all of it. I know I shouldn't have gotten frustrated but I did. Because she had a hard time trying to deep throat me, it caused her rhythm to be off. Hell, everybody knows that giving good head is about being able to keep your lips tight around the shaft, without biting, not letting your mouth get too dry and applying the right pressure and stroke.

I grabbed her head and started fucking her face hard until the tempo was right and I could feel the tip of my dick as it reached the back of her throat. She was gagging. I know, I'm sadistic but that shit turned me on more. I told her that I was cumming. She didn't try and stop me. She looked up at me as I kept going and I came in her mouth. She swallowed what she could but the rest she spit out and I started to laugh. After we cleaned ourselves off, we chilled and watched T.V. until her sister came to pick her up. She went back to school and eventually told me that she had gotten attached to me once we had sex. I really wouldn't say we had sex because we didn't have intercourse. Although I really didn't want to be with her, I felt like I had to because I took her virginity somewhat.

She would come home on weekends from school and we would fuck. I remember times when we would be having sex and I would have her blind folded because I did not want her looking at me.

Other times, I just liked to get nasty and fuck her, then pull out and make her start sucking my dick. I would move her head nice and slow and I would be fingering her at the same time, damn near having my whole hand in her pussy. I would begin to fuck her again and then just pull out and cum on her ass. Fucking her in her pussy, while fingering her in the ass was nice too. She used to let me do anything I wanted to do.

Being with her was different because we were fucking on a semi-regular basis. It felt good feeling wet pussy on my dick, hearing her faint moans, but now I felt that I had to come to terms with something I had been dealing with for my whole life, my sexuality. I had always hidden the fact that I was attracted to men, but now I didn't really care. I've accepted the fact that being bi-sexual was something that I couldn't help.

It was March when I started calling the gay chat lines. I would call them on a regular basis like it wasn't shit. When you called, they would give you a free trial membership, but there was only one free membership per household. I've devised a plan that would get me more free memberships. I'd use pay phones, my work phone, neighbor's phones, or friend's cell phones. Whenever I called the line I would never give out my real name or my phone number. I had been calling the line now for a few days with no luck; most are just wanting to have phone sex, which I would do sometimes. However, the majority of the people I had been talking to just didn't seem like my type, so I would never meet them in person.

One day I called the line, and as usual, people were sending me messages saying that they wanted to do this and that, but I got one message that was different. It was from a guy named Jeff. He just wanted to know about me and how I looked. We sent messages back and forth for a few minutes before we actually exchanged numbers and talked on the phone. He sounded like someone I could really see myself getting to know. We talked for a little bit and he asked if he could come over. I gave him my address and he told me that he was on the way. I got dressed, looking all good and everything with my wheat colored Azzure shirt, dark blue jeans, and my wheat colored Timbs. We stayed on the phone with each other until he was almost at my house, so I went outside to meet him. Next thing I know, this crazy ass Montero sport pulled in my driveway. It was silver with black leather interior and tinted windows. The window rolled down and all I see is a fine ass nigga. He was brown-skinned, wore glasses, short wavy hair, big lips, and a goatee.

"Hey," he said.

"Hey. What's up? How you doing?"

"I'm fine."

We both smiled & laughed nervously. He gets out of the car and he is a little bit shorter than me, about 135 pounds, and has a nice shape. He had on his work uniform so I asked him whether he was getting off work or on his way in. He had to be there at 5 o'clock.

"Can I come inside, Jah?"

"Yeah, it's cool. Come on in."

I guided him to my bedroom and we just sat on the bed and asked about each other's status as far as tops, bottoms, etc. There are different types of gay men as far as what we will do. Tops are more commonly masculine guys that are basically the man of the relationship, the ones who fuck. Although you do find some feminine tops, it's not too common. Then you have the bottoms, which are the ones who like to get fucked. There are also versatile tops, which prefer to be tops, but will get fucked depending on how they feel. Likewise, there are versatile bottoms, who prefer to be bottoms but will occasionally be on top. I told him that I was a top and he said he was a bottom... but we pretty much knew that already from the previous conversations we had.

"Jah, I'm really comfortable around you and I would like to get to know you a lot better."

I smiled and we held hands and watched T.V. As we're watching T.V., he starts to look at me.

"What's wrong?"

"Jah, I want you to be my first, but after I get to know you a little better."

"Are you serious? You just met me. Why do you feel like you want me to be your first?"

"Because I like you."

As he's saying this, I notice the time, "You should probably start heading for work."

He gets up, we hug and I walked him to the car and watch him leave. He called me later on that evening and we made plans to see each other later on that week. After I get off the phone with Jeff, I laid in my bed staring at the ceiling. Damn. This is fucked up. I am still dating Jasmin and just a few days ago she was at my house and I was fucking her like crazy. Now, as good as that shit felt, I'm laying here making plans to fuck someone else—a man, at that.

A few days go by and Jeff comes over while I'm home alone and he's looking so damn fine. He has on some green and yellow sneakers, khaki cargo pants, and a green t-shirt with a yellow shirt over it; talk about coordinating. He comes in, we talk for a second, and then I told him to kiss me.

"What's wrong, Jeff?"

"I'm sorry but I don't like to kiss."

"Well, that's because you probably can't."

We start to laugh and then began kissing. As we're kissing, we held and caressed each other and I start to squeeze and play with his ass. He moaned which made me want to just stop kissing and start fucking right then and there. He got on his knees, unbuckled my belt, pulled my pants down and starts sucking my dick and it is feeling so damn good. I feel my knees start to wobble a little as my body relaxed while I was enjoying the head job. He started to blow air on the tip and planted kisses on the shaft. He stood up but continued to jack me off. I pulled his pants down and I start to jack his dick too. I started stepping closer to him, forcing him to step back until his knees hit the side of the bed. I tapped him on the chest with my free hand. He sat on the bed and scooted back and put his legs in the air. I put his legs over my shoulders but spread them enough to allow me access to his ass. I am alternating

between eating his ass and finger fucking him. I then tell him to get

on all fours and I started eating his ass from the back. He had the

perfect arch in his back. I tap the inside of his thigh and he widens

the position of his legs giving me better access to his ass and nuts.

As I'm doing that, he looks back at me and asks me to cum on his

ass. I start jacking my dick and just as I'm about to cum he says

that he hears someone outside.

"Nobody is out there boy, come on."

Right after I say that, there is a knock at my window. I peeped out

and it was my mother screaming for me to open the front door.

What a way to mess up my nut!

I got up, fixed my clothes and gave him a chance to fix his and

then I went to answer the door. As I'm letting her in, she asks, *Boy,*

whose truck is that in my yard?"

"It's just my friend's."

"Uh huh," she says as she walked to her room and I went back in

mine.

By the time I got there Jeff was completely dressed, sneakers and everything.

"What are you doing? Come on. Let's finish."

"Unh unh boy. Your mama home."

"So? She don't care."

"No, I'm not disrespecting her house like that while she is here."

"Well fine then. Whatever."

We are sitting there watching T.V. and Amerie's "One Thing" video comes on and he starts singing and dancing to the music and then says, out of the blue,

"I know I can't be with you."

"Why not?"

"Because Jah, I can already see that I will be able to run all over you."

"Why would you think that? You don't even know me?"

He begins to laugh and that's when I told him that it would probably be a good time for him to leave and to call me later on that night.

I needed to call Jasmin and let her know what had just happened. Although I was nervous about having to call her, I picked up the phone and dialed her number.

"What's up, Jasmine?"

"Nothing baby. How you doing?"

"Fine. Look, I have something to tell you….we can't be together anymore."

"WHAT? Why? What did I do?"

"Nothing. I just can't be with you." And that was the end of the conversation. The next day I gave her a call to explain.

"Jasmine, I know you wanna know why I broke up with you."

"Yeah. What is it?"

"Jasmin, I'm bisexual and yesterday I had my first experience with a guy."

"Oh my God! Jah, you really cheated on me and with a damn dude? Oh my God, you are so nasty! I can't believe you are even like that."

Needless to say my feelings were very hurt because someone who I had been cool with for so long was saying these mean things to me.

We got off the phone that night and didn't talk for almost two weeks.

Meanwhile, I am talking to Jeff on a regular basis and we're making plans to see each other and spend time together since spring break was coming up. All of a sudden he acts like we didn't have plans. I'm calling him and he just brushes me off telling me that his friends are home from school and he wants to spend time with them. Me, being the person that I am, got very jealous and upset because I started feeling like I was being played with. I would call him and he would either be out somewhere eating or at the club with his friends. One night while me and Jeff were on the phone and he said *"Umm, I'm about to walk up in the club with two fine ass niggas on my arms."*

"Nigga what? Who?"

"Hakim and Martell."

"What's their last name?"

"Hakim's last name is Carlson and Martell's last name is Marin."

"What the hell? I know those dudes! I went to school with both of them since the sixth grade and I've always had my suspicions about them but never knew for sure."

I damn near flipped out. Oh my God! They are really gay.

I guess I actually said that aloud because Jeff replied,

"Yeah, they are really gay. They have both tried to get with me."

I'm sitting there on the phone blown away at the thought of Hakim being gay, especially since he was one of my first boy crushes. I got off the phone with Jeff because he made me mad by telling me he was going to the club with two fine niggas when he could have been spending that time with me.

He called me the next morning and Hakim was at his house.

"Why is he over there?"

"Why not? He wanted to spend the night. What's the problem?"

"Damn Jeff, we were supposed to be kickin' it and now you are letting a nigga that you know likes you, spend the night at your house?"

"Yeah, I don't see the big deal. We're just friends."

"You know what? Don't worry about it but please know that I ain't no damn fool. When he leaves, you can call me back."

Jeff called me back a few hours later to let me know that Hakim is gone; but, while we were on the phone Hakim came back over and lays in the bed. As we are talking on the phone I hear Jeff say, *"Not too much."*

"What are you talking about?" I asked.

"Nothing, Hakim trying to rub his dick on my ass."

"Well, he is only doing what you let him do."

"Look Jah, me and Hakim have been friends too long. I would never fuck him."

"Ok, whatever. I'll holla at you later."

A few days go by before we talk again. I've called him several times but he would never answer nor return my calls. When we did finally talk on the phone he's just being quiet, not saying anything of value. Hell, it doesn't seem like he was trying to have a conversation at all. So to break up the silence on the phone I asked,

"Did you and Hakim fuck?" Jeff laughed hysterically but did not answer the question.

"Ummm hello? Jeff can you answer the question?"

"It ain't none of your business, Jah."

"Well fine, Jeff. Fuck you and then some. Don't call me no fucking more." I hung up the phone. I refused to call him back after that. He called me every now and then but I would never want to talk, and eventually the calls stopped.

Chapter 3

On Fire, Burnin' Up!!!

I'm just chillin'. Not getting on the chat line trying to meet people at all. After that little situation I had with Jeff, I think it is best I lay low for a minute. Get my head right, ya know? I thought I had issues with women but this thing with Jeff really threw me off my game and that shit ain't cool. I have to figure out what I'm doing (or not doing) that keeps my ass drawn to these fucked up relationships. One night, I got on the phone with Lisa and one of the first things she wanted to know was if I'd met anyone off of the line lately.

"No, I'm just chillin' for a while. Right now, I'm just getting used to the fact that I'm bisexual."

"Boy, you better call that chat line and get with somebody."

We both laughed. She always seems to put things in a way that allows me to be myself but pushes me to challenge the status quo. I called the chat line on 3-way and posted my greeting.

"What up? This ya boy J, calling from Augusta. 5'6", 180 lbs., dark brown skin, low haircut, two tattoos, four ear piercing. Just sittin' here chillin', lookin' for something to get into. If you're interested hit me up."

Not even a minute later, I was getting hit with messages left and right. The funny ones were from the married white guys, who wanted to get fucked by a black guy, while their wives were at work. Lisa and I listened to a few messages and talked to a few people, but there was only one greeting that stood out to me. It was from a guy named Andre. He told me that I sounded nice and that he wanted to talk one-on-one; so we exchanged numbers and I gave him a call.

We had a cool conversation. He's a pretty funny guy. When I asked him what he looked like, he replied, *"Well J, I'm about 5'8" with light brown skin and a mini afro. I weigh like 160 and I'm muscular."*

"O.K." I said *"You sound like you look nice."*

He told me where he lived and I happened to live right not too far from me off of Barton Chapel Rd. I asked him to come over so we can meet in person. He agreed. Before we got off the phone, Andre told me that he would be wearing a wife-beater and some fatigue shorts. I took a really quick shower and then gave Lisa a call back. I told her that I was crazy nervous and asked her to stay on the phone with me while I was waiting for him to come.

For some reason, everything Lisa was saying was super funny to me. Well, until that heifer put me on hold so she could answer her other line. Some help she is being when my nerves are all out of control. I'm pacing around the yard waiting on Lisa to return to the line when I see someone wearing what Andre described as he would be wearing. I started pressing buttons on the phone and praying for Lisa to come back. She's not back on the line and my silly mood has gone full throttle towards panic mood. Shit! Shit! Shit! Shit! Shit!

As this person gets closer, I can tell for sure that it is him. Lisa finally brings her ass back on the line and I'm freaking the hell out as I say *"Look, he is coming down the street. I can see him coming."*

"First of all, breathe fool." So, I took a deep breath. *"Well, does he look good? Is he cute?"* she asks.

"I can't really tell, it's getting dark."

"Jah, when he gets closer, press the button once for ugly and twice if he's cute and three times if he is fine."

Now this person is right in front of my house and stops at the mailbox and asks

"Is this it?"

"It depends. You Andre?"

"Yeah."

"Then yeah. This is it." He smiled and I kinda chuckled to myself. One day someone is going cuss me out for being so fucking sarcastic all the time.

As he starts to walk down my driveway I pressed the button twice on the phone to signal Lisa before dropping the line. We stood on the front porch talking for a little while before I suggested we go to the back yard where we could sit on the steps… plus, there was a little more light back there and I could clearly see his face.

"You want a drink?" I asked.

"Yes, please."

When I return with the drinks, we talked a little more, just trying to get to know each other.

"Well, I have an older brother and a younger sister and I was born in Atlanta," he said.

"Oh ok. So how long you been getting down?"

"I've been gay my whole life, so I never really had to come out because they already knew." We both laughed.

"That's cool." I replied. *"As for myself, I was born in Brooklyn, New York, but I've been here majority of my life. I'm the youngest of seven kids...6 from my mother and 1 from my father... And I just recently had my first experience with a dude."*

"Get the fuck outta here! Are you serious?" he asked.

"Yep, and... I'm not out yet either. The only people that know are my best friend, Lisa, and my sister Kelly. She is bi too."

"That's what's up. Is it ok if we go inside?" he asked.

"Yea, come on."

All my brothers and mom were home but I didn't have a problem with letting him come in because he didn't look gay at all. They would think that he was just one of my homeboys. We went back to my bedroom and sat on the bed. He starts rubbing on my leg. *"Alright now! You better chill out,"* I laugh as I kid him, *"You ain't ready."* He giggles as well when he replied, *"Oh really?"*

At that, we both had to laugh. I laid down on the bed and he climbed on top of me and we started kissing and touching each other. As he kisses me on my neck, I slide my hands down his shorts and began messaging his soft, round ass and playing with his asshole. I tapped him on his ass and nodded for him to move over. Once he did, I pulled off my pants and boxers. He climbed between my legs, nestled in and started to lick my shaft while he played with my balls. He licked around the head of my dick. Ugh! I hate when someone volunteers to suck your dick but then just plays around with it.

"Stop playing. Give me what I want."

He repositioned himself, opened his mouth and swallowed me all the way to the base without gagging. Shit! He's a keeper! He is just sucking and sucking and it is feeling so good.

"Baby, I'm about to cum. You want it in your mouth?" I asked, and he shook his head yes. *"Damn, this shit feel so damn good. I'm cumming!"* I held his head so he couldn't move and I just bust all in his mouth.

"Damn nigga, you are off the fucking chain," he said after he wiped his mouth with the palm of his hand. He got up off his knees. I pulled my pants up and we sat on the bed.

"Jah, I'm getting hungry."

"Let's go up to the store and get something to eat then."

We walked up to CVS, where I worked, and all he wanted was some chips. Hell, I had chips in the kitchen. On the way, we're making small talk and he's asking me about my prior relationships and whether I liked him and shit like that.

"You're cool. I mean, I can see us kickin' it for a minute, Dre."

He smiled.

Now, we are back at my crib chillin' on the bed. We aren't really talking. Just enjoying each other's company. I must have dozed off for a second. When I woke up, Andre is staring at me and I noticed the clock's red illumination just past his shoulder that read 10:38 P.M.

"Shouldn't you be leaving? It's getting late."

"Nah, Jah it's cool. I'll go home later."

We began kissing again and taking each other's clothes off. He starts sucking my dick and I'm playing in his ass. I put his legs up in the air and begin eating his ass, as his upper body is hanging over the side of the bed. I'm tongue fucking him real good and now I'm ready to fuck him. I lifted him up and turned him over and told him to get in the doggy style position. I went and got a condom and some lube and slid my dick in his tight ass. He starts moaning.

As I begin fucking him, I'm jacking him off at the same time. He raises up and presses his body against mines and he's holding my neck. After a few minutes he finally cums all over both of our hands. I put my hand on his lower back and instinctually he removed the arch from his back. He stretches his arms in front of him and laid his head on the bed. His ass tightened around my shaft and he started moving his ass in a slow, circular motion. I might have gotten another 10 stokes in before I had to cum. That nut was amazing.

"*Damn, Jah. That shit was on point,*" he said.

"*Shit. You wasn't bad yourself,*" I answered as I slowly pulled out because I know that it would take me a while before I got my third nut.

I went to get a towel to clean us up. Afterwards we laid in the bed just holding each other and watching T.V. I then noticed that it was almost 11:30 and I said "*Maybe you should be getting ready to leave.*" He then begins laughing and I said "*What's so funny? Why are you laughing? Do you plan on spending the night or something?"*

"Yeah, I don't really want to go home," he said.

"Well, all you had to do was ask! You ain't have to try to sneak and trick me into letting you spend the night! Now, call your mom and let her know that you're not coming home." I had him do that because he was only 18 and I know that she would probably be worried about him. The next morning we woke up and I told him that he needed to leave. I mean, he wasn't my nigga or nothing, we had just met the night before.

We got up and got dressed and I gave him some money to get something to eat. I walked him to the front door and told him to call me later that night. As I am walking back to my room, Jocq and my mother followed behind me.

"What do ya'll want? Why are ya'll following me?" I said.

"Who was that? And did he spend the night?" my mother asked.

"That was my boy, Andre. And, yes he did spend the night. You saw him last night, remember?" She stares up briefly in the air. I guess she was

actually trying to remember, so I continued, *"We was just chillin' and it got late. When he called his mother, she said that it was too late for him to walk home and to stay where he was."*

My mother was like oh ok and walked off. Of course, Jocq had to be the nosey lil fucker to ask,

"Where you know him from?"

"He went to school with us."

"Well, I ain't never seen him before," he said as he turned his head to the side and looked at me with his eye squinted.

"That's because he takes regular classes and not those special ass classes with you."

"Man, fuck you. Where you know him from, for real?"

"School! You probably didn't notice him because he was only there about a month and then he left."

"That's all you had to say. You don't have to get smart all the damn time."

"If you weren't so fucking nosey, I wouldn't have to be so damn smart."

"Ha. Ha. But you still told me the answer so who is really the smart one?" he

said as he walked off.

I don't understand what the big deal is. I've had homeboys stay over before. It's almost as if they can sense that something was different about this sleep over.

I went to get in the shower and when I got out, I saw that I had a couple of missed calls. One from Lisa and several from Andre. I got dressed and I chilled for a minute before I called him back to see what he was trying to talk about. He wasn't home so I called Lisa.

"So, Jah, how was your night?" she said with a chuckle.

"It was good. He ended up spending the night."

"Wow, are you serious? How the hell did you let that happen? Did you get caught?" she said.

"Well, he kinda tricked me into letting him stay and no I didn't get caught. He actually doesn't look gay, so I didn't have anything to worry about. They just wanted to know where I knew him from."

"Damn, you a lucky bastard. I wish I can have somebody in my house without

getting caught," she said. We both laughed.

The next day, Andre phoned to say how he had such a good time the night before and to invite me a party.

"I don't know, Andre. I don't know your people like that. Besides, whose party is it anyway?"

"It's my friend's, little cousin's birthday party. They are having the party at his house."

"What?" I am NOT going to a damn children's party dude! *What the hell is your problem?"*

"The kids are only gonna be there for a little while. After that, there will be an adult's only party. All the adults are gonna be there by 8," he said.

That next day comes and Andre is blowing my phone up asking me if I'm still going to the party. I was telling him yeah, but I really wasn't sure because I didn't have a ride. He tells me not to worry about it because he's got me covered. By the time I had gotten home from work, he was calling me to say that his "gay daddy" was going to pick me up.

Sometimes, unfortunately, when people in the gay community come out to their family and friends, they are shunned. They then turn to the gay community to re-create these familial bonds. In essence, they have "gay families" which consist of mommas, daddies, sisters, brothers, etc. So I had him call his "gay daddy" so I could talk to him myself. I asked if it would be a problem if he came to pick me up and he said no. In fact, he asked Andre if he wanted him to come and get me. After we got off the phone, I showered, got dressed and waited for Andre to call me and let me know what time they were coming.

About 20 minutes later, he called and told me that he was already at the party and that his "gay daddy" was on his way to get me.

"Dre, I don't know him like that to be riding with him by myself. Why did you go before me anyways?" I said.

"Because I wanted to already be here when you got here, my bad," he said. I went outside and waited for his "gay daddy" to come. I had been outside maybe 10 minutes when a silver Neon pulled in the drive

way and a light skinned girl with kinky twist in her head rolled the window down and asked, "*Are you Jah?*"

"*Yes, I am,*" I said as I got in the backseat.

The driver, introduced himself as J-Roc, Andre's "gay daddy" and the girl was J-Roc's sister, Kendra. So we're on the way to the party, we're just making small talk and J-Roc begins to tell me how he met Andre and how long they've been friends. Then he begins asking me how we met.

"*On the chat line... a few days back. We've only known each other maybe about a week,*" I said as we pulled up to the apartment.

As J-Roc parked the car, there were some older looking guys that came up to the car and started speaking to him and Kendra and asking who I was.

"*Oh, that's Andre's friend. Where is he at anyway? Go tell him that we out here,*" J-Roc said.

I stepped out of the car and spoke to the welcoming committee.

"*Oh, shit! You look so damn good and you can dress,*" one of them said as they started introducing themselves. An attractive guy, who was obviously a bottom, introduced himself first. His name was Fred. Then, there was Byron, who preferred to be called "Paris." Then, there was another Fred and someone that I recognized, named Brian. Brian was part of the band from my school's rival. A majorette I believe.

After everyone introduced themselves, I noticed Andre coming out of a nearby apartment. He approached me with a big ass grin on his face and said, *"Hey baby, I'm glad you came. Come on, let's go inside for a minute so you can meet everybody else."*

As we walked in the door there were little kids running everywhere. He introduced me to a few more people as we made our way through the apartment. Maybe 10 minutes after I got there, all of the kids were gone and it was just me and all of the other guys that I had met earlier. We are all just sitting there chilling and Fred asks *"Jah, why you not eating? Do you want anything to drink? What's wrong?"*

"Oh I'm sorry. I'm just not hungry. I'm good. I'm just shy that's all."

The truth was, I'm new to the whole gay scene and these muthafuckers were just too gay for me. The way they were dancing was too much. Grown ass men calling each other "girlfriend" and "honey chile," that was too much. Swishing around…in public…too much!

As if reading my mind, Paris interjects, *"I know you probably thinking we're all weird and stuff but we don't act like this in public. It's just that we feel free around each other but we do respect the public."*

We all went outside and waited for J-Roc to pull the car around. We said our goodbyes. Twenty minutes later, we pulled up at my house and J-Roc announces, *"O.K Andre, I will pick you up in about an hour because you can't spend the night."*

"Why not?" Andre asked.

"Because you're not grown," he replied. *"Now, I will be back in about an hour."* We started laughing as we headed towards the front door. We walked to my room and sat on the floor and talked about the party.

"So, what do you think of my friends?"

"They were cool. I really enjoyed myself."

"Well, if you think you enjoyed the party wait until I get my mouth on you."

I am sure my face looked shocked but my body responded

instantly to his statement. He pushed me back until I was laying on

the floor. He pulled my pants down and starts to suck my dick. I

start playing with his ass.

"You need to get a condom."

"What you trying to say?" he said.

"I ain't trying to say nothing. What I said was you need to get a condom

because I don't have anymore."

"Well, if we're gonna be together, then we don't need a condom," he said. It

wasn't long before we started fucking. He was moaning and saying

that he couldn't handle it doggy style, so he laid flat on his

stomach. I got into the push-up position and continued to fuck

him. His ass was tight and it felt so good that at that time I didn't

even care about a damn condom. I felt myself about to cum and I told him.

"Baby, you can cum in me or on me, it don't matter. Just don't stop," he said.

When I came in him that was the best feeling in the world......at that time. We got up, cleaned ourselves off, and not even five minutes later J-Roc came to pick him up. I walked him outside, we hugged, kissed, and said goodnight.

After he left, I had to call Lisa to let her know everything that went on.

"Lisa, me and Andre just had sex."

"Ok Jah, that wasn't your first time so what's the big deal?" she said.

"Well, this time we didn't use a condom," I said.

"Oh my God, Jah! Are you serious?" she asked.

"Yeah, he said that if we are gonna be together, then we don't have to use one. You know I've never done anything like that before except with Ericka but that was different. She was a girl."

"You better hope you don't have nothing because I don't want to have to kill nobody," Lisa said.

"Man, come on. You know that will NEVER happen to me."

"I hope not," she replied with a bit of sadness in her voice.

"Look Lisa, it won't. I'm good. Let me take that back, Andre said I was

great." We both laughed. *"I'm tired so I'm gonna call you in the morning."*

"Ok baby. You have a goodnight and we'll talk later."

I couldn't believe what I had just done. I just had unprotected sex

with another man whom I've only known for like 3 days.

Later on that night I got a call from Andre.

"Did you have a good time tonight baby?"

"Yeah, boo. It was cool but I'm tired and I want to go to sleep... but before I

go I have something to tell you."

"Ok baby, what is it?"

"I love you," I said. My statement was returned with silence, so I

repeated myself. *"I love you Andre."*

"Ummm.......uhhhh, I don't know what to say because I don't feel the same

way. We don't even know each other."

"Oh, so you know me enough to say that we don't need to use condoms, but

when it comes to loving me, you don't know me? Cool. That's ok, I just wanted you to know how I felt. You don't have to feel the same way. We'll talk later, alright? Peace."

I hung up the phone and was so embarrassed. I didn't know how to take that. I have to admit, my feelings were hurt because of the fact that I had just opened myself up to him and he pretty much shot me down. I just laid in the bed reflecting on just another shitty episode in my romantic drama until I fell asleep.

The next morning, Lisa called and asked about the party. I told her how it went even though I really wasn't interested in talking about that party.

"Lisa, I am so stupid."

"Oh boy, what did you do now?"

"I told Andre that I loved him. I couldn't help it, Lisa!"

"Did he say it back?" she asked.

"Well, no. He said that he couldn't say it back because he didn't feel the same way."

"Look Jah, you know I love you but you fall way too fast."

I wasn't trying to hear that so I told her I will have to call her back.

I don't remember talking to Andre on Thursday but that Friday is

when I feel like the burn happened. He called me and said that he

wanted to come over. At first I was hesitant but I told him to come

on over anyways. About 15 minutes later, he's knocking on my

door. He walked in my bedroom and sat on the bed and then laid

down. I started to lay down and finish watching T.V. but he

grabbed me and started holding me.

"What's wrong with you?" I said.

"Nothing, I just wanted to hold you baby. That's all."

"You act like one of us is going somewhere," I said as I turned to face

him.

"Nah, it ain't like that. I just wanted to hold you."

I turned back towards the T.V. because after what happened that

day before, I really wasn't feeling him. I laid with my back to him

for a while before he whispered, *"Jah, look at me."* I let out a loud sigh as I turned towards him. Before I had the chance to move my head, he kissed me. His lips were soft. I really didn't want to kiss him back. I'm still pissed with him. Or, at least trying to be pissed with him but the more he kissed me, the more I wanted to kiss him back. I should have known he was on some bullshit when he said he just wanted to hold me. Hell, that's one of the oldest tricks in the book and apparently I have fallen for the okie doke again. We started kissing each other more passionately. We undressed each other and he started sucking my dick as I am eating his ass. As I start finger-fucking him in the ass, he is still sucking my dick. I then got up and grabbed the lotion and rubbed it on my dick and in his ass and started fucking him. *"Damn nigga this shit feel so good,"* I said as I forced him on his stomach while I am still inside of him. I grabbed both his wrists so he couldn't move and that made him moan even more. After I came, we both got up and got dressed then we went up to the store. When we returned, he sat for a few minutes before I walked him outside to leave because it looked like it was about to rain. As he was leaving, my neighbor was outside. I didn't really know her. I had only seen her in passing. Andre sees her and they start yelling and screaming and hugging each other like they were long lost cousins. I decided to interrupt and introduce myself because they seem to have forgotten that I was there.

"How do you know this fool?" I asked her.

"Oh, we went to school together," she said.

"Then you already know that this nigga is stupid."

We all laugh. Andre stated that he needed to leave but he would hit us both up later.

Anyways, what's your name?" I asked her.

"Oh, my name is Ebony Easton. What's yours?"

"Jah," I replied.

"Just Jah?" she inquired.

"Yep, just Jah. So, what do you know about Dre?"

"What do you mean?"

"You know what I mean. What do you know about him and what he does?" I asked.

"Oh…I know he's gay. We was just real cool in school. That's all."

"O.K. I was just asking… we're kinda seeing each other," I said.

"Yeah, I kinda figured that when I saw him come out of your house in front of you. But I never would have thought you were gay."

"Well, I'm actually bisexual. Andre is the first nigga I ever fucked with." I wasn't trying to be rude but curiosity did get the better or me… *"Ebony, are you gay?"*

Ebony is between 6'2" and 6'5", and weighed about 350 pounds; so, by her size, I automatically assumed that if she was gay, then she will be a stud.

"Uhh, kinda," she says. We both laughed.

She was telling me how she has had girlfriends before but they weren't sexual. I invited her over to my house for a while and we chilled in my room before her mother called her back home. After she left, I called Andre and I was given the runaround. His little sister would answer the phone and say *"Oh, he's busy,"* or *"he's not home."* Just bullshit ass lies. This same damn thing continued on for about two weeks.

Now, I'm vexed because during those days I didn't hear from him, I learned from Ebony that Andre is not 18… he's only 15. I could not believe that shit! A mother fucking 15 year old little boy.

A few days later, I woke up to a pair of soaking wet boxers and it looked like I had just came all over myself. I didn't think much of it until I got up to take a shower and realized that I was still having these discharges and that they were a greenish/yellowish color. I knew immediately that something was wrong and the first thought that came to my mind was gonorrhea. But, I was in so much denial about it that I was thinking it was something that was going to go away. So as I got ready for work I prepared myself for these discharges by wearing a condom to catch whatever it was that I was leaking. Periodically, throughout the day, I would go to the bathroom to change it just to stay clean. When I got a break, I called Lisa and told her that I thought it could be gonorrhea. Coincidently, she had a book with all of the STD's and their symptoms in it and my symptoms matched up with the symptoms of gonorrhea. Later on that night, we talked and she told me that she would take me to go get tested because she thought she might have something too. After we got off the phone, I called Andre so I could ask him if he has anything or if he has ever had anything… his mother said that he wasn't home. A few days later, I called again and this time his sister answered the phone.

"Hello. Can I speak to Andre, please?" Now, I put this on everything I hate, I heard him in the background saying, *"Tell him I ain't here."*

"Andre said he ain't here," she said and I hear a background full of people laughing.

"Look, little girl. I heard him in the background telling you to tell me that he ain't there. Now, put him on the phone."

"Andre, he said he heard you and he wanna talk to you," she relayed. Then I heard him once again in the background saying, *"Tell him*

that I don't wanna talk to him."

Before she had a chance to play parrot again, I said, *"Tell him I said that's o.k. I heard him. You just let him know that his nasty, infected ass gave me gonorrhea!"* As I hung up the phone, I can hear his sister in the phone saying "O*ooh, I'm go tell momma."* The next day, Lisa and I went to get checked at the health department. Lisa went in first and came out clean. Then it was my turn. I went into a room with the nurse, who questioned me about my sexual history. I explained the symptoms that I was having, like the constant discharges. She started to explain to me the testing procedure. She then asked me to pull my pants down as she pulled out a long, thin, flexi-metal rod with a cotton swab at the end of it. She grabbed my dick and just pushed it in and twisted it around. That was the most uncomfortable, embarrassing, painful shit ever. But I put myself in that situation so I had no choice but to deal with it. She then went to examine the swab. When she returned, she stated, *"Well, Mr. Marks, you were right. You definitely have gonorrhea."*

The first thing that came out of my mouth was that I was going to kill him. Well, I shouldn't have said that because she went and got me some stuff to drink that tasted like piss and then she gave me a shot in my ass. NOW, I wanted to kill the lil fucker, resurrect him and kill him again. This is some straight bullshit but I had to remind myself two things. Number One: It was my fault for being so trusting and fucking him without a condom. Number Two: It could have been a lot worse. There is a lot of shit out here that a drink and shot won't fix.

She then told me to go talk to their onsite counselor. After I finished, they gave me a brown bag full of condoms and then I was out the door. As Lisa and I were on the way back to my house, I had her stop by Andre's house because I was royally pissed and ready to fuck him up. I knocked on the door and no one answered. There were two cars in the driveway, but nobody answered.

I went home and called Ebony. I told her that it was official….I got burned.

Chapter 4

After the Burn.......

One day while Ebony and I were on the phone, she called a guy named Gary, who she said she wanted to try to hook me up with. I was kind of skeptical of her matchmaking skills since she knew Andre. Maybe this guy would be a joker too.

"*What up, Gary?*" Ebony said.

"*Shit, nuthin'. What's good wit'cha?*" he said.

"*Oh, nuthin', I got my friend Jah on the phone. I just wanted to introduce ya'll.*"

"*What's up?*" I said.

"*Hey, what's up? How you doing?*" Gary asked.

"*I'm cool. Just been chillin'... I had the day off, so I'm just relaxing.*" I said.

"*Oh ok, so where do you work?* Gary asked.

"*I work at CVS on Windsor Lakes. What about you? Do you work?* I said.

"*No, but I'm looking for a job.*"

94

"How old are you?"

"I'm 17, but I'll be 18 in October," he replied. How old are you?"

"I'm 20".

My line beeped so I asked him for his number and told him I would call him back.

When I was able to give him a call back, we were just making small talk, trying to keep the conversation going. He was telling me about how his family was from Florida but moved to Georgia a while ago. I was telling him about my family and that we moved here from Brooklyn.

"So Jah, are you an only child?" Gary asked.

"Man, please. I am the youngest of seven kids, six from my mother and one from my father. I heard that I could be like the youngest of eight. Rumor has it that my pop's first child is a girl, but no one on his side of the family seems to know anything about her. My sister said that she died when she was a baby, but I don't know. What about you?" I asked.

"Well, I'm the oldest of three. I have two younger sisters. Your mama and *daddy must've been getting' it on, huh?*

"Not really. She had three with her first husband and then three with my dad.
My dad has a daughter from a lady he cheated on my mom with."

"Oh dang," Gary replied. "Well, how do they feel about you being gay?"

"Well, one person I don't have to worry about is my father, being that he has
been dead for about 10 years. Now, my mother on the other hand, does not
know yet. I am not sure how she is going to take it. I hope she is cool and
understands. I am just starting to accept the fact that I am attracted to dudes. I
just started messing with guys back in April," I said. *"The very first person*
that I told was my best friend, Lisa, who said that she didn't care. Then, there
was and my sister, Kelly, who at the time told me that she was bisexual
also….blew my mind."

Gary and I had made plans to see each other the next day. That
morning he called me and we talked about him coming over later
on that night. In the meantime, I called Ebony and asked her to
come over. She was telling me about Gary and how she couldn't
wait for us to meet because she thinks we are really going to like

each other. I can't lie, I'm anxious as hell to meet this boy. He sounds so fine. I don't know why but at my age, I feel like I'm ready to settle down. I've only been talking to him for two days and I already know that I want to be with him.

My phone rings. I look at the caller ID and I see his number.

"Hello?"

"What's up, boo? I'm on my way to Ebony's house. You gon' come outside?"

"Yeah, just let me get dressed."

"Okay, see you in a few."

I was so excited by this time. I'm trying to get all G'd up by putting on a lavender T-shirt, light blue jeans, my white Filas with the lavender shoestrings… you couldn't tell me that I didn't look good. I called Ebony to see if she had talked to Gary but there was no answer. I go to look out my window and there is a car in the middle of the street. A guy gets out the back. That has to be Gary. As I watch him make his way to Ebony's door, she calls me.

"Ebony, is that him?"

"Yeah, we about to come outside now. Come on."

As I'm walking across the yard to her house, I see them walking out onto her porch.

"What's up, Ebony."

"Hey Jah, this is my boy, Gary. Gary, this is Jah."

"What's up?" We said in unison, and that was the extent of our conversation. Ebony and I were talking, Ebony and Gary were talking, but we weren't talking to each other. I guess he doesn't like me. Maybe he thinks I'm ugly. I'm just sitting there as he and Ebony are joking around and her mom came outside to tell her to come inside. I'm thinking that Gary is going to stay outside with me but he follows her inside. *Damn, Jah. You fucked up. You were too damn quiet*, I thought to myself.

I called Lisa and told her that I believed that I had messed up my chances of getting with Gary because we didn't talk to each other. While I'm on the phone with her, my line beeps and it's Ebony.

"What's up, Jah? How do you think he looks?"

"Ebony you know he is fine. He looks really good but I know that he don't want to talk to me because I wasn't talking to him. But he looks so damn good."

"Awwww, ok. Well, I just wanted to call you and ask you what you thought about him. I will call you back tomorrow," she said.

The next day I was at work and about fifteen minutes before my shift ended, Ebony walked through the door.

"Hey, Jah. How are you?"

"I'm good, mama. What's good with you?"

"Oh, I just got off the phone with Gary and he told me to tell you that he likes you and wants to go with you."

"Whatever, E! Stop playing!"

"No… I'm for real. You remember last night when I called you? He was on 3-way."

I burst out laughing.

"Why did y'all do that man? Did he hear everything I said?"

"Yeah, he told me to do it. He didn't want you to know that he was on the

phone."

"Man, y'all ain't right!" I said as we both laughed, walking out the door.

That next day Gary and I talked, he said he was feeling me and I told him the same. That was the beginning of our relationship. Little did I know, that relationship will be the most detrimental to me, my life, and my well-being. Dating Gary started off pretty ok. I would go to his house or he would come to mine…still, none of my family knew that we were together. I would have my brother drop me off a few blocks from Gary's house, where we would meet up then walk back to his house. Like I said, his mom didn't really approve of his lifestyle so when it was time for her to get off of work, I would have to go down the street to a friend's house, sit there, and then walk up to his house as if I had just gotten there to see him. I'm too old for this shit.

One night, Lisa, Gary, and I were on 3-way, when I had this great idea to tell my family that I was with Gary. He was trying to talk me out of it but Lisa was encouraging me to do so. I was a nervous wreck but it felt right. So while they were still on the phone with me, I went into my mother's room and I called my brother Jocq in so I could tell them. I couldn't stop laughing from being so nervous. My mother and Jocq were laughing because I was laughing. They wanted to know what I had to tell them that was so funny. Lisa was on the phone praying while Gary was trying to talk me out of it. I tuned them out as I revealed to my family that, *"Me and Neko are together."*

There was an awkward silence on the phone and in the room. My mother got real quiet and you could hear the electricity flowing through the walls.

"Who is Neko?" Jocq asked.

"Gary... me and Gary are together." He then turns to my mother, she turns to him, and then she turns to me and says *"Get the fuck out of my room!"* So, I turned and walked out.

"Jah, are you ok?" Lisa asked.

"Yeah, I'm ok."

Truth is, I really don't know how to feel. I had always assumed that she would be ok with it because she always talked about the rerun episodes of Montell Williams and Oprah, saying how a parent should love their child no matter if they are gay, straight, or crooked. So, to get this type of reaction from her was unexpected. I guess it's true that you never know how you are going to respond to a situation until you are actually in that situation.

While I was still on the phone, my mother came into my room and said *"When you get off the phone, I'm gonna fuck you up."* So, I told them that I would call them back. I went to her room and I asked her if she had something she needed to say to me.

"Just get the fuck out of my room," is how she replied.

As I walked back to my room, I was thinking to myself, is she really trying to trip on me?

I called Lisa back and told her about what happened and she asked was I ok and how I was doing. I really wanted to just give her the gist of what happened. I really wasn't into retelling the whole story so I got off of the phone. There was no way that I ever imagined that she would be reacting like this. I am her youngest child. We had such a close relationship. I swear I never saw this coming. Throughout the night, my mother kept coming in my room and just looking at me with a look of disgust. You would think she wanted to kill me. That next morning I woke up to the sound of dishes slamming in the kitchen. When I entered the room, my mother and Jocq were at the kitchen sink. I could hear them talking about me and the information that I had just laid on them the night before. They both turned around looking confused as to why I was there, then Jocq asked *"So, are you gay? Bi? Or what?"*

I said *"I'm bisexual. I'm attracted to both men and women."*

Then, my mother has the nerve to ask *"Well, I just wanna know who's the man and who's the woman?"*

"No one is the "woman" because we are both men with dicks. If you want to know who is the one getting fucked, then it's him."

"Oh, so you smackin' that ass every night then, huh?"

"Ma, don't be ignorant! I told you what it is and that's that."

Later on that day, I asked Gary to come over. He was really
nervous about coming since I had just officially come out of the
closet to my family. He thought that not only would he be the
blame but that he would be an unwelcomed guest. I assured him
that he had absolutely nothing to worry about. Boy was I wrong.

Gary came over and I walked him back to my room like I normally
would and we were just chillin', hangin' out, and watching TV
when all of a sudden I hear a *BOOM! BOOM! BOOM! BOOM!
BOOM! "Shut the hell up in there!"* at my door. I then realized it was
my mother. I opened the door and yelled *"Stop beatin' on my damn
door!"*

"Well, y'all should shut up in there, soundin' like a bunch of bitches."

I was actually confused because as far as I knew my voice hadn't
changed…especially overnight.

"Ma, what the hell are you talkin' about? All we doing is laughing."

That was all it took for my mother to go off. I know all she wanted to do was cause a scene and start a damn argument…and that's exactly what she did. She stepped across the threshold of my bedroom and just started pushing me and hitting me in my face, so I pushed her off of me. My third oldest brother, DeVaughn, comes down the hallway, trying to buff all up and gets in between me and mom.

"So, your lil bitch ass wanna hit ma? You wanna push ma?" He pushes me back with both hands.

I square up and look down my nose at him. I feel my nostrils flare as I blow out, *"Muthafucka, get outta my damn face before you get your ass beat."*

So he pushes me again. For several seconds, we push and shove each other before I said fuck it and punched him in the face. He takes a step back, put his palm to his lip, pulled it back and realized it was bloody. At this time, I squared up again waiting for him to charge me. He wiped his hand on his white t-shirt and put his palm back to his lip… I guess, wishing for a different result. The blood stain was evidence as I literally saw his lip starting to swell from the impact.

In that brief moment, I caught a glimpse of Gary sitting on the bed. He was leaned against the wall. He looked so fragile. Hopeless.

I guess DeVaughn realized he couldn't physically beat me but somehow felt that he had to hit me where it hurt the most, so he yelled, *"That's why I hope you get cum shot up to your brain and you die…I hope your faggot ass gets AIDS and die. If you like fucking niggas in the ass, then do you. Nasty muthafucka but you ain't gon' do that shit here!* As he turned to leave, he screams, *"Bitch Nigga."* With everything in me, I had to refrain from charging him after him. My biggest concern at that point was getting Gary out of here. He had seen enough.

I knew in that moment that the relationship with my family, my BLOOD, would never be the same. I felt like this was a family that

I didn't belong to; like I was just some regular ol' Joe from down the block. You know that feeling you get when someone does something to hurt you and it literally feels as if someone pinched your heart? Well, what I felt was much worse. I'm getting sad just thinking about that day.

After the massive fight I had with my family, I walked Gary home and asked him why he was crying. He said that he felt like it was his fault that my family was against me. He felt responsible for me coming out and going through all of this drama with them. I hugged him and reassured him that I loved him and he was not at fault for anything that transpired. It was gonna happen whether it was him or someone else. They didn't dislike him. They just disliked the lifestyle that they think I chose. It actually chose me.

Chapter 5

Is This Really a Relationship??

My mother told me that Gary wasn't allowed in her damn house anymore. This was unacceptable! I mean, I am paying bills there... more than she is actually paying. But if that's what she wants then I will respect her wishes...to her knowledge. There was no way that I wasn't going to let him come over. So, if he wanted to come, he had to sneak in through the window. I always kept my door locked so if someone knocked on the door then I would hide him in the closet or under the covers. When I left for work, I locked my bedroom door and left him in there; and when he felt like it was safe, he would leave through the window and walk the three blocks up to my job. Sometimes, he would go to Ebony's house and chill there until I got off work and I would walk him home. His mother actually worked so it wasn't nothing for me to go to his house and dip right before she got home. It was crazy, but hey that's love...right?

The time we spent together was nice in the beginning…especially the sex. We would just eat each other's ass and suck each other's dick to get off. We didn't have intercourse because…well, I don't know. We just didn't. We would go to the club where he would dance and I would just chill in the cut because I wasn't into the whole gay scene like that. Whenever Gary was on the floor, all eyes was on him. He could really dance. I would just sit back like "Yea, that's mines and he leaving with me." At the same time though, everyone would be looking at me because I was the new guy on the scene and I was a hot commodity. Everyone wanted me because I was the "new dick" on the block.

After we left the club, we came back to my house and his phone just kept going off with text messages and phone calls. After about the third or fourth time, I gave him the eye. I figured that would be enough for him to get the picture that this shit ain't cool. It continued to ring. I told him to tell his friends that he was with me. *"Babe, you're trippin'. My friends are probably just wondering where I am since we left the club a little early."* I didn't even acknowledge that shit. It's 2:30 in the damn morning. That ain't early. That's late. I guess he was trying to prove a point when he decided he needed to answer the next call. He actually sat up in the bed to talk to this person. When his ass sat up, my ass sat up too. I crossed my arms and stared at his mouth. I could clearly hear that it was a male's voice. I heard the guy ask *"What up? Are you with your boyfriend?"* and Gary replied *"mmm hmm."* He was polite but short to his friend on the phone. The call lasted only a minute or so. He ended the call with, *"Thank you for checking on me. I told Jah you were worried. Uh huh. Good night."* So, at that time I didn't think anything of it until I just started picking up on other little things that didn't seem kosher. He started a job at a burger joint and I was happy for him. I would get straight off work, catch the bus to his job and chill up there with him until he got off. His birthday was coming up so on his break we would talk about planning a little get together at a local bar and grille. One day we caught the bus over to Southgate Plaza because I wanted to buy a shirt to wear to his party. I got to the cash register and my damn debit card is declined. What the hell? Then, I remembered that I would occasionally let him keep my debit card when he was a little low on cash or whatnot.

"Gary, where the fuck is my money? Why can't I even buy a $10 shirt?"

"Oh, I'm sorry. I went out to eat with my mama and them."

"Nigga, you didn't plan on telling me? Better fucking yet, nigga you didn't even ask me!"

"I'm sorry baby! I'll give it back to you."

By this point I am beyond pissed the fuck off and I caught the bus back home by my damn self.

A few hours later, he showed up at my house to apologize. I was too pissed to acknowledge him. The next day we had an appointment to go and take pictures. We were planning on doing the whole dressing alike thing. It was so gay but that's what he wanted to do. Right before we were supposed to leave to go take our pictures, we got into a fight. Some guy called his phone and he was telling this random nigga all about our sex life and how he planned on turning me out. I don't understand his purpose in putting our business in the streets. Who the fuck is this dude that he feels the need to try and impress him? We don't do that shit…well, I guess I should say I don't do that shit. Apparently, Gary doesn't see an issue with it. Some things shouldn't be discussed with any ole nigga; especially some nigga I don't know. So while he was on the phone, I confronted him about it because I felt disrespected. He was yelling, saying how I was overreacting and that it wasn't that serious. I nodded my head in agreement.

"You're right," I said. *"If it ain't serious to you, it ain't serious to me. Let's fucking go. We're late for our appointment."*

Clearly, we weren't happy while we are taking the pictures and it showed on every single shot when they came back; but, by that time, we had made up and it was time to get his birthday party together. I arranged for his friends and some of our family to meet us at Applebee's for dinner. After dinner, I had the server come out with the full-sized sheet cake I ordered. It was airbrushed with rainbow colors on it. We all sang happy birthday to him. It was really nice and we had a great turn out.

After a few weeks of my mother not speaking to me and then a few more weeks of heated discussions, she finally accepted him as my boyfriend and was fine with him being over. We were chilling at my house waiting for a friend to come pick us up so we could go to the club. We both danced, laughed, and had fun that night. After we got back to my place, we undressed and got in the bed. We laid there, talked to each other, and then started kissing. That night was the first time that we made love. We kissed passionately and touched each other like never before. It felt real. Like this thing between us was meant to be. He immediately went down to sucking my dick, playing with my balls, and licking my ass, sucking my toes. We were in the 69 position, with him on top, and his ass is all over my face as I move his dick back and forth in my mouth and he does the same. I turn him around and get on top of him and slide my dick slowly in his ass. This was our first time having intercourse and it was a feeling of love that I'm sure I've never felt before. We kissed and he rubbed and caressed my back as we looked into each other's eyes. Breathing heavily, I let him feel me as I began cumming. We then changed positions and for the first time, I am penetrated. Was I nervous? Hell yea but I was willing to do whatever he wanted because I loved him…and I was compromising. As he entered me for the first time, there was a small, painful sensation but nothing that was unbearable. I was tense because I had never been fucked before but the job was done. He came and we laid there and held one another until we fell asleep. We slept in late, chilled out for a little while and walked back to his house. Although we had shared a passionate encounter the evening before, I still had in the back of my mind that he had betrayed me. So that's something that always stuck with me throughout the course of our relationship. I basically didn't trust him and what's a relationship without trust? Little did I know that this was just the beginning of all of the things that would come between us! I gave Gary a call one night and his moms said that he couldn't talk on the phone. It was weird but I just said ok.

She said *"J, he can't talk because I caught someone in my house last night."*

"What do you mean you caught someone in your house?"

"I woke up because I thought I heard something. I walked through the kitchen and saw somebody on top of Gary. I grabbed a knife off of my counter and I chased him out of my house. The first thing out of Gary's mouth was that the guy was trying to rape him. Jah, I swear I love Gary. He is my child but that didn't look like someone had forced themselves onto my son. I believe he is lying," she paused momentarily, as I envisioned the scene in my head.

"If someone was trying to rape him," she continued, *"why didn't he scream for help?"*

Another pause. My vision was broken by reality. *"Especially since I'm in the next room,"* she said. *"And… he has two younger sisters to think about that could have been put in danger also?"* she sighed. *"I just don't believe it, Jah. I really don't."*

She agreed to let me talk to him to find out what the fuck happened because by this time, I'm upset. Gary gets on the phone and wasn't really saying anything. I asked him what happened and he said that invited a guy he just met to come over and the guy tried to rape him. The voice in my head was screaming *BULLSHIT!* He must think I am stupid as hell.

"So, this guy was supposedly about to rape…"

"No supposedly, Jah. He tried," Gary interjected.

"So, again. You met some strange nigga and decided to invite him into your house, with your mom and sisters there?"

"Uh huh."

"Not once were you concerned about their safety and not one time did you try to fight this person off?"

He didn't say anything; so, hell I said it for him.

"Gary, you have to be the dumbest nigga in the whole world! Nope, I'm not falling for that bullshit ass story. NOT TODAY! HELL, NOT AT

ALL!"

So, I hit him with all the questions racing around in my head. We were going to get to the bottom of this tonight. *"Why and when did you meet this guy? Why the hell did you have this guy over your house that time of night anyway? And why did you let him in your house? What is it that you really know about him? Did I even cross your mind when you decided to let some guy come over?"*

He stuttered. *"Um. Well. He."*

Does he have a name?"

"Jah, you gone let me finish or not?"

I didn't respond.

"He called me and wanted to come over…umm, and we were outside talking. Yeah, we chilled outside for a long time but he said the mosquitos were real bad and then he asked to come inside." It's November. Ain't no damn mosquitos in November! This lie was as bad as the time he said he was going to the store and was gone two hours but didn't buy nothing.

"You can't be serious, Gary?"

The next thing I know, I heard the dial tone. This lil fucker hung up on me.

His mom called me back and asked me what I was going to do about the situation. I honestly didn't have anything to say because I was so upset at the fact that this dude is trying to play me and his moms.

The next day Gary called me mad as hell. I asked him what was going on and he told me that his mother was sending him to Job Corps. I was a little upset because that meant that we wouldn't see each other. It also meant that the trust issues that I had before were going to be worse with him being about four hours away in Albany. Hell, I was mad as fuck with him because of that so-called situation that he had the night before, but I still didn't want him to leave. I was so dumb that I was willing to overlook all the signs of him being a liar, cheater, and just an all-around crab ass dude. I didn't want him to go alone so I signed up to go with him. I had already graduated high school and was working. I really had no reason to go other than the fact that I didn't want him to go down there by himself.

Okay, I just didn't trust him enough to still be with him and let him go down there alone. Maybe I was dumb but hey that's what I thought you should do for someone that you love and want to be with. We both went to the Department of Labor and had a meeting with the Job Corps Recruiter. Two weeks later, I got a call saying that I had been accepted into the Culinary Arts program and that I would be leaving in December. I was honestly excited. I was going to be in a completely different environment, meeting people who had no idea who I was, and just kind of have my own identity outside of Augusta. I was preparing myself, telling my friends and family, letting my job know that I was resigning... just getting things in order because the program was a minimum of one year. I called Gary and asked had he heard from the recruiter and he said that he hadn't. I asked him had he called down there to check the status of his registration and he hadn't. I was upset because I had already quit my job and they had already sent me a bus ticket. I just gave up on the idea of him coming because he didn't seem interested anyway.

The night came for me to leave and his mom took me to the bus station. I was in tears the entire ride there. We waited for the bus to come. I boarded the bus and once I sat in my seat I broke down. I really didn't think that I could do it without him. While the bus was loading, all I could think about was Gary, and all that has happened in our short relationship. The lying, the possible cheating, and anything else that had happened. It just seemed like I had nothing but the entire fifteen hour bus ride time to think about all of those things. I honestly knew that once that bus pulled out, that it was over.

Chapter 6

The Beginning of the End

I finally arrived in Albany and I was not surprised by my surroundings at all. I thought Augusta was a few miles off the beaten path but this had to be one of the most country places I have ever been. I thought I was being punked. The buildings looked original, like they were built by slave labor and their accents were like something straight out of *The Color Purple* movie. There was a van at the bus station waiting to take me to campus. They searched my bags, took me to my dorm, and I just stayed up in my room until the other students got out of class. It seems like once I stepped foot out of the dorm, all eyes were on me. I walked to the cafeteria to eat dinner and there were whispers, stares, and people laughing and shit. *"Oh hell, I might have to whoop somebody's ass to prove to them that I'm not to be fucked with….if that is what it takes"* I thought to myself.

"Aye boy. Excuse me, yea you…OH MY GOD, OH MY GOD, you are so cute, do you have a girlfriend?"

"No."

"OMG, all of the boys that I was sitting with think you are so damn cute."

I'm thinking to myself ok this girl needs to calm down, however it was very flattering.

I then said, *"Well, I have a boyfriend back at home who is supposed to be joining me in a few weeks."*

"Oh ok. My name is named Alicia. Let me introduce you to everybody."

Before I could agree or disagree with her, she grabs my hand and led me over where everyone was sitting, on a wall on in front of the cafeteria. There was a line of gay guys looking at me like fresh meat. One by one they introduce themselves but there was one guy in particular who stood out named Trent. He seemed to be the pretty boy of the bunch; but he had a girlfriend even though he was out as being a bisexual male. So I respected that but I kept him in the back of my mind. Over the next few days I began spending a lot of time with this group of guys that Alicia had introduced me to. Every morning and every evening Alicia would come to my dorm to get me so that we could go and eat and just chill out and do the random activities they had on campus.

By this time, I was hearing from Gary less and less until one night I called his phone and he didn't answer. I checked his voicemail. There was a message from a guy named Andrew who said *"Gary, it's fucked up how you didn't tell me that you were still in a relationship with Jah, but you're trying to talk back to me."* My heart was beating so damn fast that I thought it was going to come through my chest. I was so hurt because the feelings that I had all along was true. He was fucking around, or at least trying to. I called him about it and he of course tried to deny that he had done anything, and that he and the guy were just friends. I told him to stop lying to me because the guy would have never said anything like that if he wasn't trying to talk to him. He told me that I was tripping and then he hung up on me. I called him back several times and he never answered the phone. The next day after class I went to the computer lab with Alicia and Omar to look at the phone records. When I pulled them up, my heart dropped to the bottom of my feet. There were several calls to the gay chat line. He had used over 3000 minutes talking to different guys on the phone. Ran the bill up to over $2,500 just for his phone line. I was pissed the fuck off. This dude that I had given my trust to, loved, and taken care of for the last few months was playing me. So I called him and confronted him about the situation. He never denied it... all he said was that he was sorry and that he would pay for his part of the bill.

"Damn right, you're gonna pay it! You are the one fucking around. I got that phone so that we can talk to each other while I was away. I'll be home in a week for the winter break. Just give me my phone back and that'll be the end of us."

He said ok. And just like that, we broke up.

The very next day, on my way to class, I called my mother just to say hello.

"Hey Ma."

"Hey Jah, how are you?"

"I'm fine," I replied as my voice started to shake.

"No, you're not. What's wrong?"

I burst into tears.

"Me and Gary broke up ma. I'm sorry for the way I treated y'all."

"It's ok baby. I know you're hurting but it'll be ok."

"Thanks ma. Tell my brothers I love them and I will call you when I get out of class. I love you ma."

"I love you too, Jah."

During our class break, I saw Alicia and told her what had happened. She said

"Well baby, just let him go. You have all of these boys on Turner that like you. Just meet someone and don't worry about that loser."

"You're right. No one here knows me and I'm here by myself. Might as well make the best out of this situation, right?"

After class I met up with Trent. He was actually waiting for me outside in the courtyard. I was pleasantly surprised. We walked and talked for a little while before settling under the gazebo to chill. He expressed how much he liked me but that he had a girlfriend. I let him know that I liked him as well and I was not trying to come in between them at all. He gave me his number a few days later as we were about to board out buses to go our separate ways for the holidays.

I had been calling Gary for a few days asking him to return my phone. I don't know why he seemed to have the impression that I gave him the phone to have forever. Hell, we were not together anymore. Why the fuck would I continue to pay for a phone, or even let you hold a phone, that I know you call other dudes with? He kept telling me that the phone was his and he was not going to give it back to me.

I went to the mall to holiday shop with my cousin and I ran into Gary's mom and two younger sisters. They asked me had I seen him because he was in the mall also. I said no, I hadn't seen him but I would like to because he needed to give me my phone back. So as we're talking and walking up the stairs, I literally bumped into him. Initially, I didn't know who it was so I just said excuse me and kept going. His sister said, *"J, that's Gary right there!"* So I turned around and looked and there he was… I instantly became disgusted. I told his mom and sisters goodbye and I proceeded to follow Gary around the mall asking for my phone.

"Jah, I'm not giving you the phone back so leave me alone."

"Please, just give me my phone. We ain't together no more. Give me my shit."

"Nope."

"Ok then. That's fine."

If he knows like I know and learned like Ericka learned, when I want my shit, I get my shit. I guess I am just going to teach his busted ass too… I don't play about my stuff. So I followed him outside the mall because he, and his friend Jessie, were about to leave. As he climbed into her car, I blocked him from being able to close the car door. He then gets out the car, pulls out a knife and runs around the parking lot trying to draw attention to the

situation. So I sat in Jessie's car and told her that she wasn't leaving

until he came back and gave me my phone back.

"J, I have to go to work. I can't sit here dealing with y'all's mess."

"Well you shouldn't have had him up here with you because this motherfucking

car isn't leaving until I have my fucking phone back."

I see from the side view mirror that Gary is approaching the car so

I got out. He got in and kicked me as I reached for the phone. At

that point all I saw was me, him, and the color red. I was about to

kill this boy. I grabbed him by his micro braids and wrapped them

around my fist and went to work on that ass… just beating him in

the face. I drug him partially out the car and began to slam the car

door on his leg. He's yelling, *"Jessie drive off! Jessie drive off…GO!"* By

that time I was already done and had gotten my point across, *"Bitch,*

you ain't gon disrespect me and my shit nigga."

During the fight he somehow ripped my shirt, so I took my ass

back into the mall, made a beeline for Macy's and bought me

another one. My cousin asked me what happened and I told her. All she could do was laugh because a couple of his braids were in the bag where I had put my ripped shirt. It was funny but I did feel bad because I shouldn't have had to fight him at all… but, I did and I would do it all over again. The real issue wasn't the phone; it was all of the anger I had built up inside of me throughout the course of our seven month relationship that I took out on him all at once. When I got home I called his mother and told her about it. All she could said was,

"I already knew what was going to happen when I saw the look in your eyes at the top of those stairs. But J, you have to let it go now. It's over. You know that me and the girls still love you. Don't worry about him anymore."

It was at that moment that I knew for sure that it was over and I was ok with that.

Being hurt and angry, I wanted answers. I knew Gary would never in a million years tell me the truth so I called Andrew. He told me everything from how he and Gary dated in the past, how he knew about us but thought that we were broken up. He came across as genuine and sincere. Andrew began calling me and we never would talk about Gary. We talked about "us." Somehow during our fiasco with Gary, we started liking each other. He was a cool dude, but on my part it was mostly about getting back at Gary. I knew what happened between him and them, and I wanted to get back at him...so I entertained it. He would come over to my house, we would chill, and he would even come and visit me at my job. We fooled around a little bit here and there, but honestly I wasn't into it, so eventually we just cut off all communication. I let that whole situation and everyone attached to it go.

Chapter 7

Because I'm Free

When I returned back to the Job Corps campus it seems the
attention magnified by 100. People wanted to hang out, chill, and
just generally be around me. I was single so I was eating up this
new attention. The one person that I immediately thought of when
I got back to campus was Trent. He was just so damn fine and to
me he looked like the singer Usher. Hair was always cut in a dark
Caesar, deep waves, and nice brown skin. Although he had a
girlfriend that I was also cool with, he and I had a very good
connection. I'm not going to lie, I did like him. But, I promised
myself that I wouldn't even go there with him because of the fact
that he was with someone. There was just something about Trent
though. He would always dress up and come get me from the dorm
so we can go to the campus store and chill; or, go to the rec room
to watch a movie or something. He was always just so nice and

charming. Trent just made me feel special and I started to develop feelings for him. One night Trent took me bowling. It was my first time ever going to a bowling alley. He made sure that I had a good time, even if it did make him look crazy. Once we got back on campus we went back to my dorm room and listened to a little music and just talked and laughed. Next thing I knew, Trent stood up, leaned down to me and began kissing me. I pulled back because I was so nervous and scared. I honestly had no idea what was happening. He tried to apologize but before he could get it out I had grabbed him and started to kiss him passionately in return. I put my hands in his pants and began squeezing his ass. It was so soft and hairy just how I like it. He got on the bed and I flipped him over on his stomach and started fucking him in the ass with my tongue. Between moans, he begged me to fuck him. I was trying not to rush this time we were sharing but I wanted to fuck him as much as he wanted me to fuck him. Now, everybody know I am a chivalrous kinda dude; so, what kind of man would I be if I didn't give him what he asked for?

I stuck my tongue in his ass once more to make sure he was good and lubed. I climbed on top of him and stuck the tip of my dick in his ass. He tightened up a little as he took a deep breath. I didn't move.

"You okay."

"Yea, it's just my first time in a long time and…"

"No need to explain. I'll go slow. Just relax."

After a second, I felt his body release underneath me.

"Yea, just like that."

I slowly slide the head of my dick in and he moaned.

"You want me to stop?"

"No. Not yet."

I started a slow stroke. His ass was so tight and warm. I really just wanted to fuck the hell out of him right now but I was trying not to hurt him.

I took several more stokes, thinking about how good this shit felt, before realizing I better slow my roll. I don't want to come too soon.

I pulled out and laid down on my back beside him.

"What's wrong, Jah?"

"Shit. Nothing. Trying not to cum," I said with a chuckle.

"Can I suck you off?"

I'm thinking what kinda question is that? You see my shit still hard as fuck. But, I had to play cool.

"If you want to."

He inched further down the bed, cradled my shaft in his hand and gave me some of the best head I have ever had.

He knew exactly what he was doing and knew exactly when to give a little more spit and when to suck the head just a little bit longer. As I began cumming, he pulled my dick out of his mouth and caught it in his hand. He then looked at it, licked it, and then we both laughed. I'm not sure if we laughed because it was just goofy and random, or if we laughed because we weren't sure what else to do. The next morning Trent met me outside of the dorm. He figured that since we were in the same trade, we could walk to class together. I really enjoyed just hanging with him. We could talk about anything and we were always joking around about something. Maybe it was because I liked him, but even when his girlfriend was around I knew that he really wanted to be with me. I wasn't going to be the reason why they broke up so I started doing my own thing. He didn't like it but he couldn't be mad.

There was this one guy named Kevin. He was tall, had a thick, solid build, nice low cut hair, and wore these hazel contacts. He and Trent were in the same dorm and Kevin kind of liked me and he had no problem making it known. He would just come out of nowhere and kiss me, or just come from around the corner and grab me and start licking on my ear and neck. Trent would be pissed the hell off but there wasn't a damn thing he could do about it because of his girlfriend, Shay. One night, we were all sitting in front of the café and Kevin came downstairs. He came and sat by us and we were just chillin'. Next thing I know he grabbed me and kissed me and started licking my ear. He told me to come back to his room and Trent stood up in front of Shay and said *"NO!"* Everyone started to laugh and Shay was like *"Well, damn Trent. Why can't Jah go with Kevin?*

"Because, Kevin doesn't even like Jah. He's just a whore." Everyone began to laugh again.

So. I jumped into the conversation like, *"Trent, are you jealous or something?"*

"No," he replied, looking as if something stank. *"Why would I be jealous? I have a girlfriend."*

"OK, then." I turned and started walking towards Kevin and we began walking to his dorm. I had no intentions of going to his room or even going to the dorm, I just wanted to make Trent jealous. I told Kevin that I couldn't do it and we began laughing. I guess he got the unmentionable joke.

Later that night, Trent approached me right before curfew and asked if we could talk.

"Jah, you know you were wrong, right?"

"For real? How was I wrong?"

He looked at me as if I were speaking a foreign language.

"I'm being serious, Trent. What did I do?"

"I dunno," he replied. *"What did you and Kevin do?"*

"Not a damn thing. I just did it to piss you off. You know I am not feeling him like that."

"Uh- huh. You know that shit ain't cool tho."

"Why are you trippin'? I thought you weren't jealous."

"I'm not," he said as he diverted his eyes. *"I mean, maybe. Maybe, I am just a little jealous,"* he admitted

"Just a little?"

"Ok, a lot…. Damn, Jah. I…" he let out a deep breath. *"I like you a lot. I really do. I want to be with you. Like for real."*

"Then, what's the problem. I mean, besides Shay."

"Truthfully?" He had to laugh at himself. *"I forgot who I was dealing*

with. Of course you want the truth."

I nodded.

"The truth is Shay is just a smoke screen."

"What? You're tripping."

"No. Seriously. I care for Shay but she is really just a diversion for my family. They don't accept my lifestyle and it is easier to take home someone they are comfortable with than to make every damn holiday uncomfortable for everybody because they don't approve of who I love.

"Does Shay know this?"

"Do she need too?"

I didn't know how to answer that.

I explained to him that I could definitely understand where he was coming from because of everything that I had gone through with my family; however, I was not gonna settle for being in the background. Trent and I continued being friends but the feelings grew stronger and stronger…on both sides. He was sneaking out of his dorm after curfew just to come see me. He still wanted to walk me to class. On the days when he didn't have a class in my building, he would still walk all the way to class with me and then be late to his own class. I loved the attention but I wanted more. I was in love with him. He wasn't willing to break up with Shay so I had to move on.

When I first got to campus there was this guy named Roderick. He was sexy as fuck too. He was kind of light brown skinned, had a nice beard, braids past his shoulders, and he was about 5'6"-5'7". I heard that he got down, but I wasn't too sure and because I couldn't confirm it I never made a move.

A few weeks after I decided to cut my losses with Trent, I walked in my room but before I could get my key in the lock good, my roommate opened the door and hurried me inside the room and closed the door behind us.

"Chris, what the fuck is your problem?"

"Nothing girl. Just read this note," he said as he pushed a sheet of spiral note paper in my hand.

First of all, there is something wrong with his strange acting ass.

Secondly, I hated when he called me that! I am nowhere close to

feminine. At all! But, that was Chris, with his overly gay, dramatic

self. To him, everyone was a Chile, Honey Chile, Bitch or a Girl. If

I didn't know better, I would think he didn't know anyone's real

name and used those as fillers.

The note read:

What's up, Jah?

I've seen you around campus and

you're not like the other gay guys out here.

I want to let you know that I like you.

Signed, Rod.

Barely containing my laughter, I said, *"Chris, get the fuck out my face*

with these games!"

"Girl, I'm not playing. You know I would not even play like that. You do

know who that is?"

"No. Am I supposed too?"

Chris opened his locker and out walks Roderick. I damn near pissed on myself.

"Man, y'all get the fuck outta here. Ya'll play too damn much." By this time, I was laughing hysterically because I couldn't believe it. *"Is this real or a joke?"*

Rod came to me and put his finger over my lips to shut me up, then he grabbed me and kissed me. Those lips were so big and soft. Normally, I don't like facial hair on a dude, but on him it was nice…I loved it.

He then pulled back and said *"I like you but I'm DL so whatever we do, we have to keep it on the low."*

"Are you serious? Is this real dude? What the fuck?"

He gave me his number and then snuck out of me and Chris's room. I was still stuck. I couldn't believe what had just happened. This guy didn't look like the type that would pay me any attention.

I guess that was probably my insecurities but from that moment on, we did share something.

He would come down to my room every night to talk and say good night. He would call me every morning to say good morning and if no one was in the hallway, we would sneak a kiss. I felt like a kid at Christmas every time I saw him or got a chance to talk to him. Of course, since he was DL, we never did anything publicly. If we would happen to pass each other on campus, we would dap each other up; but, hold each other just a couple seconds longer than we probably should have. He would call me after class and want me to come up to where he was just so we could sneak a little time together. He would order lunch and instead of me going to the café, he would want me to eat with him. Most times we were in there alone, so that was our time to be together. Trent called and asked why I wasn't in the café because he was waiting on me. I told him that I was at the front gate eating lunch with someone. Rod and I were just sitting there talking and the next thing I know Trent is busting through the door. Looking pissed off, he asked, *"What are you doing in here with Rod? What's going on with y'all?"*

Rod immediately jumped up and said *"Man chill out! We're just talking about some shit that happened in the dorm. That's all."*

I just stood there in amazement at how quick he came up with that lie. I then dapped Rod up and told him to hit me up later on and I walked out with Trent.

"What's wrong with you Jah? Why were you with him? Is he gay?"

"Ummm, no. At least I don't think so. I have never asked him. But why does it matter, Trent? Last time I checked, you had a girlfriend."

"It matters because I like you. I mean, Jah, I love you but I can't break up with Shay right now. Look, can we just hang out later… after class?" I told him yea, and then I walked back to my class.

Later that evening Trent met me in front of the dorm. He was dressed…differently. Normally he is very clean cut, nice pants with a collared or button-up shirt tucked in, and some type of casual shoe. This day he had on some baggy shorts, sneakers, and an all-white tee. I stepped outside and said *"OK Trent. This is different. What's going on?"*

"Nothing Jah, I can dress like a boy sometimes." We both laughed. We walked around campus talking and sharing laughs. Trent then suggested that we walk behind the pool hall.

"What are we doing back here?"

"I want to suck your dick, Jah. Please?"

I pulled it out as he got on his knees and began sucking my dick. Trent knew how to work a dick. He used his hand to jack me off as he was sucking the head, getting spit all over the place. He then stopped and told me to let him know when I'm about to cum because he wanted to see me nut. About two minutes later, I pulled out and he told me to start jacking off. As I came, he then gave me this little sneaky grin and got back on his knees and went to work. I guess the risk of being behind the pool hall and possibly getting caught was enough of a turn on to allow me to cum again. But, a funny thing though, after that night things between Trent and I became a little strained. Actually, things got kind of bad because I wanted to be all or nothing.

Later that night, Rod came down to my room and asked me what was going on between me and Trent. I just told him that I was Trent's little secret because he wasn't going to break up with Shay. Once those words came out of my mouth I knew I had to do something, but I kept quiet.

"What are you thinking about baby?" Rod asked.

"Nothing. Just trying to figure out what I'm going to do with myself."

"Well, I know what you can do with me. Meet me in my room tomorrow night" Rod said.

"Ok, I sure will."

He kissed me and then left. I got in the shower and just climbed in my bed and went to sleep. I woke up to someone kissing me and rubbing my head. I opened my eyes and it was Rod.

"When did you get back in here? How long have you been here?"

"Not long, I just missed you and wanted to talk but you were sleep. I didn't

want to wake you but I couldn't help myself. I had to touch you."

I was still in and out of sleep as he was talking. Then I heard Chris

say, *"You better get out, Rod. I hear the RA coming."* He then kissed me

again and he left. Being that it was after curfew, everyone had to be

in their own room. So now I have feelings for a guy who has a

girlfriend and another guy who is DL. My life at TJCC was getting

pretty hectic.

I tried to talk to Trent and he just kept walking as if he didn't see

or hear me. *"Trent. TRENT!"* I called out. He kept walking. I

brushed it off as maybe he just wasn't having a good day or

something. Maybe someone pissed him off. Later on that evening

me, Shay, Kevin, Bryce, Cedric, and Omar were sitting on the wall

in front of the café just chillin' and talking. Trent came and sat on

the other side of Shay, who was sitting next to me. All of a sudden

we just hear this growling sound. Everyone starts to look around

and the focus turns to Trent. He's sitting there gritting his teeth

and growling like a rabid dog. Everyone looked at me like I had done something. Everyone wanted to know what the problem was and what was going on with Trent. He continued growling the entire time… never saying a word. The rest of us continued our conversation and then headed in for the night. I went into the dorm and at that moment I decided to just let it all out. I had made up my mind that I was going to tell Shay EVERYTHING that happened between Trent and me.

Chapter 8

...And So It Begins

I told a few friends about the things that had happened between Trent and I and how he's becoming this asshole. He doesn't want to have to share me but I am supposed to be okay with having to share him. I told them that I planned on telling Shay and everyone advised me not to do it. I said fuck it. It's not my relationship and I know for damn sure that Trent can't whoop my ass, so why not tell? I was walking across campus with Bryce when I saw Trent and Shay under the gazeebo. It was now or never.

"What's up, Trent? Why aren't you talking to me? What's the problem?" He just sat there staring into space not even acknowledging my presence.

"Ok Trent. Do you really want to play like that?" He did not respond. *"Cool."* I turned to Shay.

"I just want you to know that me and Trent have been fucking around behind your back for months. He's sucked my dick several times and I've eaten his

ass. We've gone out off campus a few times and the only reason he's with you is because his family doesn't approve of his lifestyle."

Everything just got quiet. Shay looked at Trent.

"Well, is it true Trent?"

Trent never moved from that spot nor did he answer the question. Then he looked at me and stood up. *"Really, Jah? I can't believe you did this! You're so fucking stupid!"*

"NO, YOU'RE THE FUCKING STUPID ONE MOTHERFUCKER!" I yelled as I walked up to him. At that moment, a friend of mine named Jake ran up from the other gazeebo and got between us. He grabbed me and told me to come walk with him.

"No! No, Jah! I don't want you to get terminated. Trent is not worth it. Trust me." Jake said as he looked back over he's shoulder. It was well known on campus that Jake didn't like Trent anyways. Only a few of us knew it was because Jake had a crush on Shay. *"Jah, look at you! You will kill that boy,"* he said with a laugh. That was the last

night that I would ever speak to Trent on campus. He changed trades so we never saw each other in class anymore. Maybe a month or two after that, he graduated and went back home to Atlanta. I often wished I hadn't done that. I really did love my friendship with Trent but how he was treating me just wasn't fair. I never had the chance to apologize or ask him to forgive me for being so childish and acting out of hurt.

A few days after Trent left, Shay came up to me and said that she wasn't mad at me for messing around with Trent behind her back and that she understood why I did what I did. Then she said, *"Jah, you know what's funny? I knew he liked you. One weekend around your birthday, we went to the mall and he bought you all kinds of stuff, jackets, t-shirts, and everything. He said that he was doing it because you don't have a lot of stuff which I know is a lie because you can dress. I knew he did it because he liked you but then he told me that he was taking it all back because you made him mad. I didn't understand it, but now I do and I forgive you."*

"Shay, this is all new to me. I never knew that but please, again accept my

apology."

We hugged and went our separate ways. Not long after that conversation Shay graduated the program as well. I never spoke to her again.

After all of the dust settled down from that little situation with Trent and Shay, I kind of just chilled out for a while. Me and Rod still talked and often messed around. One Saturday night, when we had late curfew, he invited me to his room. I was friends with the Resident Assistant on duty so she didn't trip that I was on the floor to hang out with Rod. Generally, being on a floor where you did not live was forbidden. Rod and I just chilled and watched movies. He wanted me to take his braids out for him. I loved doing that because he had a very nice grade of hair so I loved playing in it. When I finished, I just stood in front of him, leaned down towards him and we just kissed. Rod was one of the best kissers I have ever encountered... even up until present day. He then stood up and we were holding each other and kissing. I slid my hands down the back of his pants to play with his ass.

Then there must have been a shift change because there was a big knock at the door and it was a male RA named Mr. Hill, who tried to come in the room. Rod hurried me into his locker and tried to keep the RA from coming in. He must've known what was going on because he was just laughing hysterically at the door and then he left. Once he left, I came out of the locker and Rod and I stood by the bed. He pulled my pants down and began sucking my dick. While he was sucking, I grabbed his head with both hands and just moved it slowly back and forth while playing in his hair. He stood up and asked me to fuck him. I turned him around so he was facing the bed and told him to get in doggie style. I stood on the floor behind him. I started to finger his ass hole to loosen him up. His ass started to get wet. I attempt to put my dick in and he jumped. My head wasn't even all the way in.

"Damn, Jah. I'm sorry. I can't take it. I've never been fucked before." I bent over and began tongue fucking him. The more he moaned the

more turned on I got. I began sucking his balls. He arched his back like he was about to cum. I stood up and summoned him to me. We kissed while jacking each other off.

"Rod, I'm about to nut. Damn nigga. I'm cumming." Right as I said that, I started jacking my own dick and I shot my load all the way to the other side of the room on the other bed. *"Daaaaaaaamn Jah! Oooh shit! That was sexy as fuck nigga."* We both laughed. Not long after that, I snuck out of the room using the side stairs and went back to my floor. After that night we still continued to see each other and speak but not as often as before. We kind of just drifted apart. After Rod, there wasn't really anyone else that I really wanted to deal with on campus. Omar was sexy as fuck, but we were more of friends with occasional benefits. I began getting on the chat line in Albany and meeting guys. There was this one guy that hit me up named Demontay. He was a cool dude and he lived not too far from the campus; so he was someone that I saw myself hanging out with on the weekends. We talked a lot, then he wanted to meet

up so I said cool. He and his Aunt came to pick me up from campus. The first night we actually met in person, all we did was just chill and watch movies. He was an all-around cool dude so I knew we would get along. But, I also knew, we just met each other so I knew there wasn't going to be any sex involved. The more we talked the more we began to like each other. I had been to his house several times on the weekend. His aunt wasn't much older than us so she was cool and didn't mind coming to get me off campus. He wanted me to come over so when I got there, we headed straight to his bedroom, as usual. He wanted to have sex. From the beginning, Tay knew that I was a top and he was cool with that. He took his clothes off. I took my pants off and he began sucking my dick. I was nervous because there was a house full of people and anyone could walk in at any time.

"Don't worry about that shit. Hurry up… I want that nut," Tay said. I nutted in his mouth. He looked at me and smiled, then swallowed it. I was turned the fuck on by that. Maybe 15-20 minutes later, Tay

was sucking my dick again.

"Tay, let me get in that tight ass man. I'm ready to fuck."

"No. I just want that nut in my mouth again. Come on. Give it to me." he said. I busted a second nut.

"Damn man. You're trying to dry me out?" I asked as I laughed.

"Naw, man. But that's my dick nigga. I can suck it as much as I want." He continued to suck me until his mouth started to get dry.

"Hold up."

"What's wrong?"

"Let's chill a minute." We sat up and watched the tail end of the movie that had been playing this whole time. We decided to take a little nap. I woke up to Tay sucking my dick, again.

"Dude! Come on! Are you serious?"

"Yes, give it to me man," he said.

This was the third nut that he was getting out of me within a few hours and I can't lie, that shit felt good. After I nutted, he then asked me to suck his dick. I was like cool, so I began working that shit, sucking the head, using nothing but mouth and tongue.

"That's how you suck a dick," he said. *"Let me nut on you. I want to get in that ass."* Tay said.

"You trippin'! You already know I'm a top and I'm not trying to get fucked... but, you can grind on me if u want to... just to get a nut."

As he was just sliding his dick up and down between my ass cheeks, he attempted to actually go in my ass.

"What the fuck are you doing nigga?" I said as I tensed up.

"Nothing. My bad." He kept grinding on me, holding me by my wrist, as I laid on my stomach. The next thing I know he is inside of me and thrusting hard and fast.

"Get the fuck off of me, Tay! Stop. MOTHERFUCKER STOP!" I screamed.

He continued to penetrate me and it was one of the worst pains in the world. If you're not prepared for it then it's not an enjoyable feeling. I was rocking side to side trying to shake him off of me. Then, he got up. As soon as I got up, I knocked the hell out of him.

"Nigga, what was that for? Come on. You are exaggerating. It wasn't that bad," Tay said.

"I fucking told you not to do that shit AND I told your simple ass to stop. Take me the fuck home."

He told his aunt that I was ready to go back to campus. The whole ride there I was quiet. I got out the car and didn't even say bye. I walked from the front gate to my dorm, got in the bed and cried. Omar came in the room *"Heeeey Jah, where you been? Mmm, you been off campus. You was being a little hoe,"* he said with a laugh. Omar saw that I wasn't laughing and he came and laid beside me on the bed.

"Oh my God, Jah. What happened? What's wrong?" he asked.

"He forced himself on me Omar. He wouldn't stop and when he finished he thought that it was a fucking joke." I said.

"Are you serious?" he said as he began to hold me. *"I've been in this situation before. When I first came to Turner, I met someone off campus and was raped too. You need to go to Wellness and tell somebody up there so you*

can go to the hospital," Omar said.

He went and told the RA and there was a security van waiting on me at the front of the dorm. There was a little old lady in Wellness and I couldn't even talk. She just grabbed me and hugged me. When I arrived at Phoebe Hospital I told the nurse what happened and they immediately took me to the back. I had to go through the embarrassing rape exam, where the nurse stuck long, Q-tip looking tools up my ass... and then her finger. Then two detectives walked in, a Caucasian lady and a Hispanic guy. The lady wanted exact details on what happened so I had to tell it to her all over again. Then, the heifer had the audacity to ask, *"Wow, you got three orgasms? Someone like you is rare."* They both laughed as they walked out. Soon after, the Hispanic detective came back in and handed me his card. He wanted me to go over my story again. So, I did. Then he stated, *"Well, in the State of Georgia, there is no such thing as a man being raped so I kind of find this hard to believe."*

I said, *"Excuse me? I was raped. I told him to get off and he wouldn't. I told him to stop and he didn't. Are you trying to tell me that because I'm a fucking man that it's impossible to be taken advantage of?"*

He stood up. *"We will be in touch."*

That was the first and last time we spoke. Nothing else was said or done and I was pissed. I couldn't believe what he had just told me. Is he for real? I thought.

A few days after that incident, Tay called me and asked why I felt the need to get the police involved. He also offered a half-assed *"I'm sorry."* I hung up on him and never had any contact with him after that.

There were few people on campus that knew about what happened but the one person that helped me get through it, besides Omar, was my Student Government Advisor, Ms. Shedlock. She was like the mother of the campus. She took care of everyone and you could confide in her and trust her to not judge you or spread your business. Ms. Shedlock was an open-book as well. She shared stories of real life that actually helped and motivated any and every one she encountered. A very strong woman she is and no matter how long we go without talking I can still pick up the phone and call her. She calls and checks on me too. There were also my close friends that I called my sisters, this singing ass girl name Ciera and my other "sister," Shenya. Everyone was just so supportive of me during this time. It was this circumstance that caused me to know that I had family for life in these people. One person I surprisingly grew close to during this time was the President of the SGA, Alicia. She was an interesting girl. She could be just as girly as some and just as thugged out as most. I found that very attractive. I have no idea how we became so close, but we suddenly started hanging out, eating together, and spending a lot more time together than we normally would have. I knew she was dating this guy named Kevin, who was from her hometown, but she was always all up in my face and told me that I didn't have anything to worry about.

One night we all went out for her birthday to some club. After a few drinks, me and Alicia were on the stairs tonguing each other down nonstop, for what seemed like the whole night. I honestly don't even remember how we got back to campus. I walked in my room drunk as hell. I figured it was best I sleep this shit off. I fell onto the bed, clothes and all. The way I am feeling right now, I will probably have the mother of all hangovers in the morning. Omar came in shortly after I did. He took his clothes off and lay next to me on my bed. I was in between being sleepy and drunk as hell when I felt Omar pull my dick out my pants. It didn't take very long of him giving me head for my shit to get real hard.

"Omar, no. I'm too drunk man. Let's do this tomorrow."

"No. Fuck that, Jah. I've been wanting to ride this dick for a while."

Without further warning, he just started riding me. *"Now I got it. Oooooh, shit! Give me that dick, Jah,"* he's saying as he's moaning lustfully.

Not even two minutes later I bust a nut.

"Really, Jah? You gon do me like that? That's some bullshit."

"Omar, I'm sor…" and that's all I remember. I'm not even sure how

I got from his bed onto mine.

The next morning, Alicia met me in front of my dorm and we went to the campus store. Unbeknownst to us, her so called boyfriend was there as well. As Alicia and I walked by, he stood up.

"Where were you last night? And who put those hickies on your neck and chest?"

"Kevin, I'm grown. You better get out of my face," Alicia said as she walked behind the counter to come sit with me. He walked out pissed off but he couldn't do anything. He damn sure couldn't whoop my ass. Later that day, me and Shenya were headed to the pool to chill. As we were walking up the sidewalk, Kevin was coming down and he stopped me.

"Jah, what's going on with you and Alicia?"

"What do you mean? Can't you tell? She's my girl, nigga."

Shenya stepped in. *"Come on, Jah. Let's go. You done took this boy's girlfriend. He finna beat you up."* I laughed and told her that she didn't have anything to worry about because I could definitely hold my own. Kevin proceeded to walk away. I never talked to Alicia about the situation because it wasn't really anything to tell.

Later on that week, we went out to the club again and met some friends at the hotel for some drinks. It was me, Alicia, my homie (who I called my auntie) Cookie, Ciera, and an ass of other people. I don't even know whose room it was. All I remember is someone giving me a drink and I was dancing on the sink. From what I was told they had to hold me up and hold my dick so that I could use the bathroom. They said I threw up in the tub... I was a mess. I think someone put something in my drink. That next morning I didn't remember where I was but I woke up next to Alicia and that's all that mattered. We were cuddled up under each other in the bed with Cookie. We started kissing. Then hands started going places... parts of my body started waking up and it was about to be on. I slid under the covers and began pulling her panties down to start eating that pussy and the next thing I hear is a toilet flushing and someone coming out of the bathroom. *"SHIT!"* I said out loud.

"Ooooh, y'all was finna do the nasty," Cookie said.

"Shut up, I thought you was still in the bed," I said.

I guess everyone else in the room woke up when they heard us talking. When I got out the bed to wash up they started talking about how much of a fool I acted. I felt horrible. I went to the bathroom and there was throw up all in the tub… the only thing I recognized was pieces of chicken.

We got back to campus and I went straight into the dorm and went to sleep. I don't even think I came out the rest of that weekend. On Monday, I saw Alicia walking around with some random guy. I didn't pay it much attention. It was kinda the norm since Monday was when the new OT's (new students) came in. By Alicia being the President of the SGA, she was one of the ones who would greet the new students and give them a tour around campus. As usual, after class we all met up in the SGA building with Ms. Shedlock, just to get some stuff planned for the student store, things on campus, as well as different things for the community. Alicia brought the dude with her to the meeting. Now, that was strange. He just came in, sat down, and didn't say much. Alicia introduced him as "Fiya," which was pronounced like fire. Over the next few days I really didn't see Alicia much. I could never seem to find her around campus.

While eating in the café alone one day, Danielle (who was Omar's cousin) called me over to a table to sit with them.

"Hey Jah, what's going on? Your girlfriend is in here." she said.

"Where is she because I haven't seen her in a couple of days?" I asked.

"She's over there with her new boyfriend. That's why she's been avoiding you." Danielle said.

"Man, whatever. Get out of here."

"No, Jah. She's for real. Look! She's coming in now," said Omar.

I looked to my right and yea, she was coming in with Fiya.

"Alicia…Alicia, come here," I called out. She just kept walking like she didn't hear or see me. So I walked over to the table where they

were sitting at and sat right next to him.

"What's up, man? What's going on?" I asked.

"Ain't nothing new," he said while trying to avoid eye contact with me.

"So, what's up with you and Alicia? That's your girl?" I asked.

"Yea, we go together," he said.

"Oh really? Alicia is this true?"

"He's my friend… yes," she replied.

"No, is he your boyfriend?" I asked.

She didn't answer the question. I got up, dapped Fiya up and told him I appreciated his honesty. I walked away. After that Alicia and I acted like that moment never happened. We just went our separate ways. We never discussed it or anything, it was what it was.

Chapter 9

That's My Youngin'

After my situation with Tay, I was a little jaded with Turner Job Corp so I put in my request to leave the program early. Because the police were involved, the incident was reported to the head of the campus. They laughed in my face so it was like being slapped after being raped. Yea, the place that I had come to, the place that was supposedly here to help and guide the youth, didn't do anything. Well, I take that back. Because of the incident, they did grant me permission to leave early with my full Culinary Arts trade certificate. I guess they figured they agreed to educate me not protect me. So, all in all I got what I came here for.

Because I knew I was going home soon I wanted to have someone waiting on me when I got there. I never wanted to go a moment without being with someone. I called Lisa and told her to keep her eyes opened for someone who would be a good match for me. She knew all about my sexual escapades and likes and dislikes when it came to my mates. I was almost done with the program and only had a couple more months left.

I was coming from the gym one day when I spotted a tall dude with a hoodie on. I have never seen him on campus but his mere presence piqued my interest. I didn't know his status but something about this moment told me that it was irrelevant. I always felt like I could get anyone I wanted so he was no exception. I started asking around and found out that he was single and gay. This dude had no idea who I was or that I even existed. He was completely clueless to the fact that he was about to be mine. Whenever I saw him, I would just stare him down. I didn't make it a secret that I liked him; nor, did it take long for word to get back to him, because a few days later, he came (as expected) looking for me. I was sitting in front of the café when he and his friend came and sat down too.

"I heard you've been asking questions about me."

"You've heard right. What's your name?"

"I'm Dantez. And there is no reason to introduce yourself. I know exactly who you are. Everyone around here knows who you are."

I chucked. *"Is that so?"*

He chuckled too. *"Mmmm hmmm. They call you the OT Whore."*

I damn near choked on nothing. What kinda fucked up introduction is that? I mean, just because it seemed like every week I was with a new boy, they assume I'm a ho. Hell… they were all just fuck buddies. It wasn't that serious but this nigga didn't know me like that to repeat that shit. Anyways, I laughed it off.

"My name is Jah."

He extended his hand. We shook. I asked him how old he was and he told me that he was 19. We exchanged numbers. Before he had even walked away good, he text me: Nice meeting you. I smiled. From that point on, we talked or texted every spare moment of the day.

It was early afternoon on a Saturday that we decided to meet in the courtyard to hang out.

Because people were always milling about campus on the weekend, we ducked off behind a building just to get some alone time. I stood against the wall with one foot propped against it. Dantez stood in from of me, with both palms on the wall…almost like he was doing a push up while standing up. He said he wanted to play a game called "Do You Prefer?" He said it's something he made up to get to know me better. I said ok.

"Do you prefer Batman or Superman?"

"Batman."

"Ok. I like Superman. Do you prefer mornings or nights?"

"It depends."

"That's not how the game goes," he replied jokingly.

"Naw, seriously. I like mornings because I like cereal." We both laughed.

"But, I love nights because I find it hard to sleep so I stay up watching reruns." He gave a face that said, 'Get the fuck outta here.' I shrugged my shoulders.

He said, *"I am a morning man myself. I tend to give the best head in the morning."*

I fanned myself as I cleared my throat. He laughed.

"Ok. So…Do you prefer to be hugged or kissed?"

"Kissed… if the person is good at it."

He laughed again. *"Why you always gotta add extra shit to it, Jah?"*

"Because these are hard questions, man!"

He chuckled. *"Well, I will make it easier."*

I raised my right eyebrow. *"What does that….?"*

Dantez kissed me.

You know how in the old movies when a dude kisses a girl and it's real good, how her foot pops up behind her? Well, my foot was already up so I collapsed against that wall. That kiss was everything and sealed the deal. He was my first official boyfriend on Turner. From that point on we walked around holding hands and were damn near inseparable.

I was really into him and I know he was feeling me but Dantez had a lot of "friends" and that shit got on my last nerve. Not because he had friends but more so because they were fakes. They were just using him. People called him "The Rich Boy" because he was extremely generous. He was getting all these flaky ass muthafuckers cell phones. Friends were even asking me *"Jah, can you ask your boyfriend to get me a phone?"* Bitch no, I thought to myself. I had to tell him, *"Look Dantez, these people aren't your friend."* Soon enough it all stopped and I was happy.

One night Dantez snuck me into his room so we can fuck and I was ready too. The lights were off, he was sucking the hell out of my dick when his roommate walked in. *"Oh my bad, I'm sorry y'all,"* his roommate said. Dantez didn't skip a beat. He just kept going. Shortly thereafter, we heard the RA on the floor so we had no choice but to stop.

"I have an idea. Come with me." He followed me down the back stair case and across the court yard. Since it was after curfew at this time, we moved in the shadows of the trees and campus buildings until we reached our destination.

"Omg, Jah! Are you serious? The SGA building?" he asked.

"Man, shut up before someone hears you. Just come inside," I said. I opened the side door because I know that door didn't latch when it closed. We went through the bathroom into the main area. I sat down on the couch and ordered him strip down. Without a further command, he spit on my dick and then started riding me. He was bouncing up and down, rocking back and forth, while looking back at me. Twice leaning back to kiss me while still riding. That boy know he knows how to work my dick.

"Fuck, Dantez! I'm about to nut," I said.

"Give it to me, Jah. Bust that nut in my ass baby," he replied. As soon as I came, it was like my body got numb. We both just sat there while my dick was still in his ass. He leaned back and kissed me and I just held him. He got up, we put our clothes back on and snuck back out of the building and went our separate ways to. Later that night, he text me and told me that he loved me. I felt like I had a million birds in my stomach, not butterflies but birds. I got so anxious and

excited and told him that I loved him too. That next morning we met in the café for breakfast and just talked a little bit before we went to our classes. I couldn't stop smiling or thinking about him. That was my baby. Every chance we got, we were in that SGA building; fucking on the couch, fucking on the floor, fucking standing up. We didn't care….that was our personal hotel room. It felt good loving and being loved, for once, and I didn't want it to end right away.

One day we were in our spot behind the academic building and he had his hand in the pocket of his hoodie. We were just playing around and I grabbed his hoodie and his Turner ID came out of his pocket. Dude was a yellow card. Now, let me explain this. On Turner, everyone had an ID card that told your age. Red cards were anyone 21 and older. Blue cards were students from the ages of 18-20 and yellow cards were anyone under the age of 18. So naturally when I saw the ID I grabbed it.

"Dantez, what the fuck is this? You're only 17 years old dude?" I asked.

174

"Jah, please don't be mad," he begged. *"I knew if you knew the truth about my age, you wouldn't want to talk to me and I really liked you."*

"Man, we could've been cool. For real. But I can't mess with you like that. YOU ARE SEVENTEEN Dantez! Seven-fucking-teen! Who does that? Who lies about their age?" I asked.

"SOMEONE WHO DIDN'T WANT TO LOSE YOU! THAT'S WHO!" he screamed.

By this time, I am pacing back and forth. Every few steps I would sigh. What the fuck do I do now? I care for him but he's 17. Seven-fucking-teen! How the hell did I end up once again falling for someone so young? I stopped dead in my tracks, closed my eyes and started to mentally talk to myself... *"Jah, just fucking calm down! You know that once you leave Turner it's not like you are ever going to see him again. It's not like you knew his age and just went along with it all this time. HE LIED TO YOU! It is almost time for you to graduate the program anyway. You are going to enjoy the rest of your time on campus...whatever that means. You're not going to trip about this shit. Everything will be fine."*

When I opened my eyes, Dantez was gone.

When I finally talked to Dantez later that night, I let him know that I decided that we would kick it. I failed to mention it was only until I left. Then, I will put all this behind me but in the meantime, why should I have to literally jack off the rest of my days on campus when I can let him do it for me. After all, he does it so well. Nevertheless, a few of us decided to make a run to Walmart. Once we got there, Dantez ran off to one side and I went to the other side. I was on the phone with Jasmine and Bre'yanna.

"Jas, you know I'm coming home in a few weeks. You gotta hook me up with somebody."

"What boy? Don't you already got a boyfriend? Where he at?" she said.

"He's in Walmart with me but I kind of ducked off so I can talk to y'all," I said as I laughed.

"He's gonna come around the corner and kick your behind," Bre'yanna said laughing.

"He gonna go all Ike Turner on that ass," Jasmine chimed in.

"Fuck ya'll. I'm trying to be serious and ya'll heifers are playing."

"We listening, Jah. Damn," said Bre'yanna.

"Jasmine, you sure you don't have no gay friends you went to Atlanta Job Corps with? No gay cousins? Nothing?" I asked.

"Ewwww, why you wanna talk to one of her cousins and y'all used to go together?" Bre'yanna asked.

"Girl, it is perfectly fine. That does not matter to me" Jasmine said laughing.

"See Bre'yanna, mind your business," I said as I laughed. *"So, come on Jasmine and hook me up with somebody,"* I said.

"Alright, Mark's dang," she said. She always called me by my last name when she got aggravated.

"Well y'all, I gotta go and feed my baby. I'll talk to y'all later," Bre'yanna said.

"Ok, bye," Jasmine and I said almost in unison. Bre'yanna dropped the line.

"You gone hook me up for real?" I asked.

"Nigga, I already told you yes. As a matter of fact, I'm at my grandma house and you can talk to my cousin. He gay."

Without any further warning, a male voice said *"Hello."*

"Hey. What's up? Who is this?" I asked.

"Who do you want it to be?" he said.

I couldn't help but to bust out laughing. That line was so funny and corny to me.

"Boy, what's your name?" I asked.

"Lance. What's yours?"

"It's Jah. Nice to meet you Lance. I know it's short but I have to go. Do you have a cell so I can hit you back later?"

Lance proceeded to give me his number and then we hung up.

I met back up with my Dantez and we paid for our stuff and left.

As soon as we got back to campus and put our things away, I called Dantez and asked him to meet me at our spot. I know I had only talked to Lance for a hot minute but I kept hearing his voice in my head. It was strong. Almost melodic and for whatever reason it turned me the fuck on.

I envisioned what it would be like to undress him. To lick his ass and finger fuck him. To hear him moan my name. To massage his head while I fucked his mouth. To take control of him. I commanded him to the floor and I held his legs as they were pushed back over his head. His ass was so damn good and tight. I wanted to cum but I resisted. The feeling in my entire body was heightened as I rammed his ass and he matched me stroke for stroke. As my dick is sliding in and out, his name slipped past my lips. Lance. I didn't break my stroke but panic hit my mind. Did Dantez hear it? I looked down at his face and he looked so sincere. His eyes were closed so I damn near shouted, *"Baby, I love you."* I wanted to be sure he heard that. He bit his lip. I slowed but never stopped my stroke. I wanted his ass to feel the love. I put Lance in the back of my head and gave Dantez all of my attention. Although I knew we didn't have much time left together, I wanted him to remember me. Since his young ass wanted to play with me, I plan to leave his ass feigning for me after I am gone. After I nutted in his ass, I stayed in for a second. I wanted him to catch every drop of it. I then got up and reclined back on the couch. I told him to crawl over on his hands and knees. As soon as he reached me, he started sucking my dick while jacking his. I gotta be honest, I think that was the best sex that I've had on Turner and I will probably be thinking of his ass when I get home… Well, unless Lance turns out to be as promising as I hope.

That next day Dantez and I talked about me leaving.

"Jah, I don't want us to stop talking because you're leaving. I think we can make this work" he said.

"How is it gonna work? I'm sure we will still talk occasionally, but you know damn well we aren't gonna see each other again." I said.

"Let me come home with you. I live in Atlanta. That's only two hours from Augusta," he said.

"It's not going to work, D. Let's just accept it for what it is."

Later on that day, I called Lance and we talked for hours. We hit it off really well. We had some of the same likes and were both Aquarius's. He also went to Turner and had only left a few months before I got there. The more we talked the more I began to remember him from high school. He graduated two years before me but I remember him from seeing him and Jasmine together. The more we talked, the more I began to like him. Less than a month after meeting him, we decided we should throw our dice into this relationship. By the time we made it official I had cut Dantez completely off. I told him that I was coming home to Lance. He didn't like it but he didn't have a choice. There was just no way that we could keep our relationship going. Every time I talked to Lance, he was just as excited for me to come home as I was. I couldn't wait to get to him.

Chapter 10

This Is It

As I made my rounds to say goodbye to my friends, reality set in that I was finally leaving this place after ten months. Dantez was emotional because he knew that this would be the last time that we would see each other. In the days preceding, he tried to go to the business office to see if he could leave with me. Luckily that attempt was shot down.

Omar, Ciera, Bryce, and Sheyna all walked with me to get on the security van that was taking me to the bus station. Ciera and I hugged, as we cried our goodbyes. I told everyone that I loved them and that I would talk to them soon. The door closed and that was it. I was officially done with Turner Job Corps.

I called Lance crying because I was sad to leave these people who had become family but I was also happy to get home to him. While I was on the phone with him, I called my mother and let her know who Lance was and introduced them. She kind of gave a dry hello.

I wanted her to know the name because we were going to be

together for a long time...I could tell.

Getting home on that bus seemed like the longest ride ever. It took

about 15 hours total because we went from Albany to Atlanta;

then, there was a layover before disembarking in Augusta. I got

home and called Lance and he could barely contain himself. *"Oh my*

God! My baby is home. I want to come see you but I work late and I don't

want to be funky. But I can come see you tomorrow."

"It's ok, baby. I'm home for good. I'm not going anywhere. Tomorrow would be

fine." I said as unpacked my clothes. I took a shower and laid down

in my bed. It felt so good to be home. That next morning, Lance

called me about 7:30.

"Hey baby, did I wake you?" he asked.

"Naw, I was woke. Just laying here. What's up?"

"Oh nothing, I just dropped my mama off to work and I wanted to come see

you but I got my niece with me."

"That's cool, ya'll can come thru," I replied.

"Ok, I'll be there in a minute."

I jumped out of bed, washed up and got dressed in record time. I put on my brown tootsie roll t-shirt, some dirty denim jeans, and my wheat Timberland boots. I was fresh all before 8am. I refused to see my baby and not be at my freshest. Not to mention this was our first time meeting in person, so I felt a little pressure to kind of impress him. I went outside and waited for him. A few minutes later my phone rang.

"Hey, what's up," I said.

"I'm just turned on your street. How far do I come down?" he asked.

"I'm the 5ᵗʰ house on the right past Brookshire," I answered.

"Oh, I think I see you. Oh lord. You're all dressed up and I'm looking like a bum."

He slowly pulls into the driveway and he steps out of the car. My heart begins beating faster and faster. I was nervous as hell, but I had to play it off.

"Hurry up and get your short ass out the car," I said laughing.

"Hey baby, so what do you think? I know you think I'm ugly, right?"

"Lance, shut up." I grabbed him and kissed him, *"You are not ugly. Come on. Let's go in the house. It's too cold out here."*

He grabbed his niece and we walked in the house and went in my bedroom.

"So, what do you think? Are you satisfied with what you see?" I asked.

"You look good. I'm very satisfied" he said.

We both laughed and proceeded to watching TV and playing with his niece. He didn't stay long but it was good finally meeting him face to face. I knew that he was the one… for sure.

Lance and I spent every moment together. We were always going out to eat, to the movies, shopping, the park… just doing things that couples do. The first night Lance stayed over we had sex. It was so passionate, we just kissed and hugged and held each other. I laid him on his stomach and I spread his ass open and stuck my tongue deep in his hole. The deeper I went the more he moaned.

He got up and began sucking my dick. I held his head and started

fucking his mouth like it was his ass. It reminded me of the time I

was thinking about him while I was fucking Dantez. By that time, I

was ready to fuck him for real so I threw him on the bed, laid him

on his stomach and slid right in his ass.

"Ooooh shit, Jah. It's been a minute… go slow," he said as he tensed up,

which forced my dick out of him. I was slowly sliding it back in

and he was backing up on it helping to ease it in. I started taking

slow, shallow strokes to get him accustomed to me. As soon as we

got in a rhythm, we were good.

"Jah, this shit feels so good. Damn."

I responded by going deeper and harder. He moaned.

"You ok?"

"Yes. Fuck. Me. Please?" he said between deep breaths.

His ass fit around my dick like a hand in glove. I would slowly take

my dick out and slowly put it back in just to feel his ass squeeze the head of my dick.

"Damn, nigga. I'm about to cum," I said.

He grabbed the bed with both hands like he was bracing himself, then I nutted. I got up and started playing in his ass while he jacked his dick until he nutted. His body shuddered.

"Shit. I just got hard again watching you cum."

Without saying a word, he got up, pushed me in the spot where he was and started sucking my dick. I damn near lost my mind. We were the perfect sex partners, probably because we really loved each other. My family loved him and surprisingly my mother called him her other son. That was a big change from just a year prior. Lance practically moved in because he stayed with me every night. He would come over when he got off at night, take his shower and get in the bed…he was home.

We loved each other's company but there was one thing that we agreed we needed to change ASAP. The size of my bed. It was a twin size bed. We are two grown ass men sleeping in this little ass bed. My mother made a joke one day saying *"Y'all can't sleep together if y'all mad, y'all gone turn over and still be touching."*

We laughed hysterically even though we all agreed she was telling the truth. So, Lance and I went out shopping for a new bed. We finally choose a queen size bed. After we got home from shopping we talked about getting our own place. We both had decent jobs and figured it was about time... the truth was we wanted to be able to fuck in every room and we couldn't do that at my momma's house. I called Lisa and I told her that Lance and I were planning on getting our own place. She asked would we mind having a roommate. Lance loved Lisa so he said it was cool. We made plans to go looking at places later that week.

Later that night while we were sleeping, my phone rang. I sat up in the bed and rubbed the sleep out of my eyes. The clock illuminated 1:34 a.m. I answered the phone and a voice said *"Jah, wake up. It's Craig."* I hadn't heard that name in almost a year. Craig was one of the guys that Alicia introduced me to. He wasn't on campus long as he was terminated shortly after I got there. *"Craig? What's up? What's going on man?"*

It is always assumed that when someone calls you in the middle of the night, it is always something bad.

"What are you doing calling me so late?" I asked.

"Well I'm in the club…."

This nigga is drunk dialing me? What the hell?

"That is nice to know," I said, *"But, me and my boyfriend are in bed."*

"You didn't let me finish. I was going to say I found someone that wants to talk to you," Craig said.

Who the fuck could that be? I am sure whoever it is, I don't want to talk to them. I hear the phone rustling.

"Hey Jah, it's me Trent. How are you?" he said.

I sat straight up in bed and just smiled. *"Trent, oh my God! How are you?"* I asked.

"I'm good, I just wanted to tell you that I love you so much. I'm gonna get your number from Craig and I'm going to call you ok?"

I just smiled and said *"Ok, get your drunk ass off the phone and I love you too,"* I said laughing.

"Ok Jah, I love you," Trent said and then the line disconnected.

I couldn't believe I had heard from him.

"Who is that you're telling you love them?" Lance asked.

"That was my friend Trent from Turner."

Lance knew who Trent was and the extent of our relationship. He knew that there would be nothing between us. That next morning we met up with Lisa to go looking at apartments. The first place we looked at was ok, but we didn't like the setup. The second place we all fell in love with it. It was very spacious and we all could definitely afford the $615 per month. The master bedroom had two separate closets and its own bathroom. The second bedroom wasn't as big and the closet was the size of a coat closet, but enough for one person. So we filled out the applications, paid our deposit and just waited for the call to let us know if we were approved or not. While we were waiting we decided to go out and eat. About an hour later we got the phone call: *"Congratulations, you guys got the apartment. When would you like to move in?"* the leasing manager asked.

"Are you serious? We got the apartment y'all," I screamed to Lance and Lisa. I didn't care that I was in the middle of a restaurant. I was excited that I was going to finally move out of my mothers' house and in with my boyfriend and best friend. Initially when we looked at the apartment Lisa begged and pleaded for the master bedroom and we said that it was cool. Well later that night I started thinking about it. Lance and I were going to be paying two-thirds of the rent and by it being two of us, obviously we wanted to have our own closet. So I talked to him and he agreed. I called Lisa to let her know that we decided to take the master bedroom.

"That's not what I agreed to Jah. I need that separate closet for my work uniforms. Plus that other bathroom is open to the hallway. If we had guest, I don't want to share a bath with them nor do I want anyone seeing me when I shower."

"Lisa, what are you talking about? No one will be able to see you because you have to go around two corners to get to that bathroom and its right next to what would be your bedroom."

I started to get mad because I felt as if she was being a spoiled bitch. So what we had initially agreed that she can have the master bedroom. I have a right to change my mind.

"Well, that's ok, Jah. I just won't move in with you guys and I'll tell her to take my name off the application." she said.

"Ok, that's fine," I stated, then we got off the phone.

The next day Lisa called me. *"Jah, I called the leasing manager and she said that you and Lance's credit isn't good enough to get the apartment on your own. So, if y'all want the apartment then y'all have to let me get the master bedroom,"* she said.

"Lisa, it's not that big of a deal. If you don't want to take the smaller room then it's fine. We can find someone else."

There was silence on the phone and then Lisa hung up. I called the apartment manager and asked her would Lance and I be able to keep the apartment without Lisa and she said no. So I called my cousin Allura and told her what was going on. Before I could get everything out she said that she would move in. I was ecstatic. So that same day Lance and I met up with Allura and her boyfriend Jamel at the manager's office and she applied. The manager came back about 15 minutes later with an approval. We all jumped and screamed. It was a very happy moment for us all. I text Lisa and told her that we got the apartment and didn't need her. That was the last time I heard from Lisa for a few months.

Allura, Lance and I moved in right away. We didn't have much but what we had was ours. Allura and I both worked at SITEL so sometimes we would ride together. Lance worked less than five minutes from the apartment, so it was convenient for everyone. Occasionally we would invite some friends over from work and I would cook for everyone. We were enjoying living together.

One day while at work and I got a phone call from Omar.

"Hey, Jah. Where are you?"

A Kaleidoscope of Love

"I'm at work, on my break. What's going on?"

"Go somewhere and sit down. I have to tell you something," Omar said.

"Boy, stop being dramatic. What is it?"

"It's Trent. He's dead" he said.

My body got numb and I couldn't move. It's like everything started happening in slow motion. *"Stop lying,"* I said tears streamed down my face.

"You know I wouldn't lie about that," Omar said.

"What happened?" I asked.

"Him and this guy he was dating, or used to date, got into an argument and dude stabbed him."

I couldn't believe what I was hearing. Trent couldn't be gone. This couldn't be true. We had talked just a couple of months ago and the last thing he said to me was *"I love you."*

"Are you gonna be ok, Jah? I know y'all had y'all issues before he left Turner," Omar said.

"Yea, we've talked since I've been home. Everything was good."

194

"Ok. Well, I just had to let you know because regardless of the issue y'all had, I know y'all loved each other. I love you, ok? Hit me up if you need anything."

"Thanks, Omar."

I was still in shock, just stuck because I couldn't believe that Trent was gone. I couldn't even focus. I had to leave work.

That night Lance was trying to comfort me. I wasn't crying anymore. I was just sad. I was just having flashbacks of us at Turner, all of the times we laughed, the arguments, and also our last encounter and I regretted it so bad. But I felt good knowing that we had at least spoken to each other and said I love you. That gave me a lot of comfort.

Not long after that my cousin Allura decided to move out. There wasn't any bad blood or anything. She just had a lot of bills and it ended up being a little overwhelming for her, and I understood. Even though she moved out she still covered her part of the rent and we really appreciated that. So now that Lance and I had the place to ourselves we had even more fun just enjoying being a couple and enjoying life. One morning I woke up with an idea…I want to propose to him. I talked to Allura and Lance's sister, Lacy. They were both supportive. Next, I needed to devise a plan to get it all together.

First, I ordered Lance and me some wedding bands online from Walmart. They were nice, sterling silver bands. Secondly, I told him that I was stressed and need to get away so we planned a trip to Orlando, Florida for a week. I wanted to propose to him right before we left for our "vacation." Next, I suggested we should have a party. I invited my friends. He invited his friends. I secretly told everyone what my plan were, except Lance.

The day of the party I ordered a sheet cake from Walmart that was airbrushed with colors of the rainbow that read: *"Lance, will you marry me?"* I loved it. I hid the cake in the closet of the spare bedroom. We took a shower, got dressed and people started arriving. I called his sister Lacy into the room to show her the rings and she loved them. So as the party is going on Lance has no clue that I'm going to propose. I was so nervous. I went to the spare bedroom and walked out with the cake. Lance was sitting at the table with his back turned to me. I came around the corner and everyone began to clap.

"What the hell is going on?" Lance asks as he's turning around.

"Lance, we've been together for five months now. I love you and I don't want to be with anyone else…Will you marry me?" I said as I sat the cake on the table before him and got on one knee.

"Oh my God, are you serious? Is this for real? Come here boy! Yes, I will marry you," he said.

I didn't even have a chance to get the ring out the box before he grabbed me and kissed me. Everyone then began cheering and clapping. It was so surreal. At that moment, I felt that I was the luckiest man in the world. I had just proposed to my best friend and I couldn't wait to see where life would take us…This is it.

Check out an excerpt of my upcoming book, *Out of Turn*.

- J.R. Mack

Got Me Messed Up

"Ugh, I can't believe that it's raining on our vacation," I said looking out the sliding glass doors. We had just gotten to Orlando and it was storming.

"Yea," Lance responded. *"Hopefully it's not like this the whole week. I can't wait to check out Universal Studios and Island of Adventures."*

"Me either," I replied, *"but by the look of the skies, we won't be venturing out anytime soon."*

We decided to make the most of this indoor time. We ordered a pizza, watched TV, and just chilled on the balcony watching the rain for a little while. It felt great just being able to unwind and know that we didn't have any obligations that we had to attend too. All we needed to do was enjoy each other's company. We

showered and got into bed. We were both tired from the trip.
Although it was still fairly early, we figured we would call it a night
and hopefully, weather permitting, start our vacation tomorrow.
I tried to sleep but it seemed that I could not find a comfortable
position. I tossed and turned. I tried laying close to Lance but I got
too hot. I tried laying on my side, which was closest to the air unit,
but I was too cold. I tried propping up and I even tried to lay flat
but nothing seemed to work. I just didn't get it. Lance is on his
belly, sound asleep. Shit. Now, what do I do? I got up to pee and
get a soda from the mini fridge. I sat on the foot of the bed and
turned on Channel 9 News to catch the weather report. I turned
the sound down as not to disturb Lance. The meteorologist stated
that the rain should be clearing out and the rest of the week looks
amazing. Just what I needed to hear.

"Babe, are you coming back to bed."

I looked over my shoulder and Lance was still laying in the same
position.

"It depends."

"On what?"

"Can I have some?"

He started laughing. He pushed back the covers to reveal that he was nude underneath. I guess he had taken off his pajama pants and boxers while I was in the bathroom. I placed my soda can on the dresser and climbed back in bed, on top of him. I started kissing the back of his neck while I grinded on his ass. He started rotating his hips beneath me.

After a few minutes he asked, *"Why are you teasing me, Jah?"*

I chuckled. *"Never that. I just wanted to make sure you were ready."*

"The better question is are you ready?" he said with a chuckle.

I bit the back of his neck. *"Let me show you."* I sat up on my knees and tapped him on the ass. He pushed up into doggy style. I started tongue fucking him. Once I felt his body relax, I put my dick at the rim of his ass but didn't enter.

A second later he pushed back until my entire shaft was in him and he started bucking against me. I held his ass for support. I didn't dare move. It felt too damn good and I didn't want to throw off his rhythm. I started cheering him on. Telling him how sexy he was and how great it felt. He started bucking harder. I slapped his ass and the very next buck, he abruptly pulled away.

"WHAT THE FUCK?" I yelled.

He didn't say a word. He got up off the bed and tapped for me to sit down on the edge of it. I felt like a child whose balloon just popped. What kinda sick ass game is he playing? Lance pushed me on the chest until I fell back on the bed. As soon as I did, I felt the warmth of his mouth around my penis and instantaneously, I came. I couldn't help it. I laid there as my body convulsed. I have never felt anything that explosive in my life. He straddled my now limp dick but I could feel the blood start to gorge again…Can I possibly be this hard, this quick?

I can feel and smell cum as Lance started to kiss my neck, my cheek, my forehead and the corner of my mouth.

"Stop playing before I fuck you again."

"Is that a threat or a promise?" he said as he stopped to look at my face.

I gave him a sly grin. He quickly climbed off me and put his ass in the air. It was mine for the taking. So, hell, I took it.

After a couple hours of erotic play, Lance and I laid cuddled in the bed.

"I still can't believe that you proposed. How did you get all of this by me without me finding out?" Lance asked.

"I'm just good like that homie," I joked.

"I'm just glad that I was able to pull it off man. You don't know what I went through to make sure those rings were here on time and to make sure you didn't find out about the cake. But I'm glad you liked it."

"Yea. It was the sweetest thing anybody has ever done for me."

"It's only the beginning." He smiled.

The rain let up and we decided to take a walk on the strip. There were a few restaurants, bars, and souvenir shops. There was a pond that had fake alligators in it with bright lights that reflected off of the water to make it look like they were moving. The whole scene was just nice and romantic. It felt good to get out of Augusta for a change and do some adult shit like enjoy a real vacation.

The next two days were spent at the theme parks. By the third day, we were exhausted and our feet were killing us from all the walking and standing in line. I was tired from my vacation and surprisingly ready to get back to Augusta. The fourth day was spent touring the city by bus and picking up a few souvenirs to take home. We did have friends there that said that they were going to come by but the only one that came was Aunt Cookie. She bought a pair of her friends. We all sat around, drinking and talking shit. The next day, we had breakfast at the hotel before catching the shuttle to the bus station. We came back home and life was back to normal.

No sooner than we got back, I ran into Antoine. I met him through Gary. He was very slim, light skinned, low cut wavy hair, and an all-around cool dude. We became friends but we never really hit it off like that. His mother was too strict and I was a grown ass man. I didn't have to listen to her but unfortunately he did. A few days later, he sent me a friend request on MySpace. We messaged back and forth for a while and come to find out he lived in the apartment complex behind the one I lived in. So after asking Lance would he be ok with Antoine and I hanging out sometimes, we made plans to see each other and just chill.

I made a point to schedule a visit when I knew that Lance would be home. Since it had been about three years since I last saw Antoine, we spent the time just catching up. It had gotten late so he asked could he spend the night. Before I could even get anything out, Lance looked at me and said that it was ok. So he got up and went to get Antoine an extra blanket and a pillow. After Lance left the room, I looked at Antoine and asked *"Why do you need to stay the night? You live like maybe a ten minute walk from here. It's not that bad."* He just looked at me and didn't say a word.

The next morning, I walked Lance to the door because he had to go to work. As soon as I opened the door there were these two big bags under the stairs that lead outside.

"Antoine, are these your bags out here?" I yelled.

"You mean the bags under the stairs?"

Is this negro trying to play me? *"Yea, the two bags under the stairs."*

"Ummmm. Yeah. They're mine," he said. Lance just looked at me and laughed. *"That's your friend. You deal with that mess."* We both laughed and I kissed him goodbye.

"Antoine, come here please. Why do you have bags outside my front door?" I asked. He peeked past me outside like he didn't know the damn bags were there.

"Oh. See, the truth is, my mom put me out and I need a place to stay. I was hoping that you didn't notice them. I didn't know Lance had to work or I would've hidden them a little better." he said.

"What the hell do you mean? I know damn well you don't think that you're moving in here with me. You're out of your rabid ass mind if you think I am moving you, or anyone else, into the apartment that me and my fiancé share.

NOPE. Not going to happen," I said as I slammed the door.

"Jah, it's nothing like that, and it won't be long…" before he could even finish I cut him off and told him that he needed to find another place to stay by that night.

Throughout the day there was a little awkward silence in the house. We would make small talk but nothing serious. It was just crazy how this guy that I had only seen in person twice, thought that it was ok to just move himself into my apartment.

Not that I really wanted to know the answer, but I needed accurate details when I relayed this bullshit to Lance, I asked, *"So what's up? Why do you need a place to stay?"*

"My mother doesn't like my lifestyle," he replied matter-of-factly.

Hell, my momma didn't like my lifestyle but she didn't put me out. I impatiently rolled both hands in a circle to give him the indication to go on. Let's get all this bullshit out in the open.

"Well, she told me that as long as I want to become a tranny, I cannot live under her roof."

My eyes got big. *"Excuse me…tranny? So you want to become a woman?"* I asked.

"Not right now but eventually I do."

"Well, get the fuck out of here. I wasn't expecting that…at all, but ok. If that's what you want to do, then go for it. Your mother doesn't have to accept you but she does have to respect you."

Once Lance arrived home, we all sat down to eat dinner. Before we could even get our first fork full, Antoine just came right out and asked *"Lance, can I move in with y'all? I'm having a lot of problems at home and really don't want to go back,"* he said.

"Well what's going on?" Lance asked.

As Antoine is telling him this saga, I am shaking my head and squinting my eyes at Lance like your mother would do when she's signaling that you better not embarrass her in public.

"Jah, what's wrong with you? What's wrong with your eye?" he asked.

"Really Lance! Are you kidding me?

"Ummm, yea Antoine, I guess you can move in. But only for a little while

though. This is not a long term or permanent situation," he said.

All I could do was get up, put my plate on the peninsula in the kitchen and go to the bedroom.

"What's wrong with you?" Lance asked as he followed me to the bedroom.

"Why did you do that? You know damn well I was telling you to tell him that he couldn't stay and you go say some crazy mess like that 'what's wrong with your eye'. Like for real?" I asked.

"Well you know how I am. I just want to help people."

"Fine, whatever. You just didn't have to throw me under the bus like that. And for the record, you told him he could stay, he is now your problem," I said. Lance looked at me strange. *"Mark my words that one is going to be trouble."*

"Babe, don't think the worse. He just needs a little time to get his head together and figure out his next move."

I pursed my lips and walked off.

OK. Maybe I was wrong but as I was leaving for work the next day, I felt the need to lay down the house rules like my momma did. So I told Antoine that he better not mess up my house, he better not have anyone in my house, and he better not order shit on my T.V. or my phone…and that I would see him when I got off. I wanted to leave it positive. When I got to work, I told all of my friends about what happened and they all laughed hysterically. I didn't find it to be funny at all.

A few days go by and we are still in this awkward situation. I had gotten in the bed early because I had to work the next morning. As soon as I dozed off, Lance came in the bedroom and said *"Jah, get up. I need to talk to you…NOW."*

"What is it, babe. I'm tired."

"Come to the kitchen," he said as he turned to leave. I sucked my teeth, got up and walked to the dinette table to sit down. Antoine was already sitting there. Lance stood with his arms folded.

"Now Antoine, tell him what you told me," Lance said angrily.

Antoine hesitated for a moment. He looked at me, then at Lance and then back to me.

"Well, I told him how you've been trying to sleep with me, Jah."

Now, it was my turn to look at him, then Lance, then back at him.

I am not believing my ears.

Antoine continued, *"...and that Lance needs to leave you because he deserves better. Much better. Lance is a good guy."*

I didn't even get mad. I just sat there. *"Really Antoine? You're just going to sit there and bold face lie like that?"* I said. *"Please tell me when and how have I been trying to sleep with you? Remember, I work and when I'm not working, we are here with Lance. You are the one who came here and blatantly lied just so you could try to move into my damn house. You know damn well I haven't tried to do anything with you."* Then I turned to Lance, *"You're stupid as fuck for believing his ass. Antoine get the fuck out my house."* I got up and walked back to the bedroom because I didn't have time for the crazy mess. I had money to make and they are disrupting my beauty rest on some bullshit. I turned around and Lance was behind me.

"So, it isn't true?" he asked. *"Hell no! And you know that. Think about it. Why else would he come here with his bags if he hadn't already planned this? He's trying to fuck shit up and it ain't happening. He needs to fucking go!"* I made sure I said it loud enough for Antoine to hear it.

Before leaving for work the next morning, I called Antoine into the kitchen. *"I don't appreciate what you tried to do last night. We tried to help you but that was just some shady ass shit. I need you to get your shit and get the hell out of my house."* Lance stood there and nodded in agreement. We walked back to the bedroom and Lance apologized and said how he should have never believed Antoine from the beginning and asked did I forgive him. Of course I did. I would have probably done the same thing. As a matter of fact, I'm sure if someone came to me and said that Lance was trying to fuck them, I would have fought him first and then asked questions later. While we were talking, I heard the front door close.

I go to the kitchen and I see a handwritten letter from Antoine.

It read: *"Jah, I really am sorry. I know that you are mad at me.*

Hopefully you can forgive me. I was wrong for what I did.

Maybe one day, I will have what you and Lance have.

Signed, Toine"

I took that letter and threw it away and that was the last time that I ever seen or heard from Antoine. From that moment on, I knew that I had to be aware of the messy gay dudes in Augusta.

Nobody Knows

So you say that you know me, but you don't know me at all.
What have I been through? What am I going through? What is it gonna
take for me to get you to understand I ain't the same as I used to be? Just
because you see me in a magazine, or on your TV screen, that doesn't
mean that I'm always happy, nobody knows.

Nobody knows I don't want to be alone. Nobody knows, nobody knows
the things that I've been through. Nobody knows, nobody knows the
things that I've seen. Nobody knows, nobody knows the real me but me.

Yea you might see me with nice things, but material things don't make
me. They don't give me hugs, they don't show me love, and they are not
there when I am feeling lonely. Just because you see me with a little
money, and everybody knows me, I'm still same ol' J from around the
way, but nobody knows.

Nobody knows I don't want to be alone. Nobody knows, nobody knows
the things that I've been through. Nobody knows, nobody knows the
things that I've seen. Nobody knows, nobody knows the real me but me.